Y0-AGK-520

STORIES
of
CONNECTICUT

Lively Tales of The Past

by

Longshaw K. Porritt

with

Heimwarth B. Jestin   Ruth D. Maher

Copyright© 1992, TXU 477637

Published by

Hitchcock Printers
191 John Downey Dr.
New Britain, CT 06050

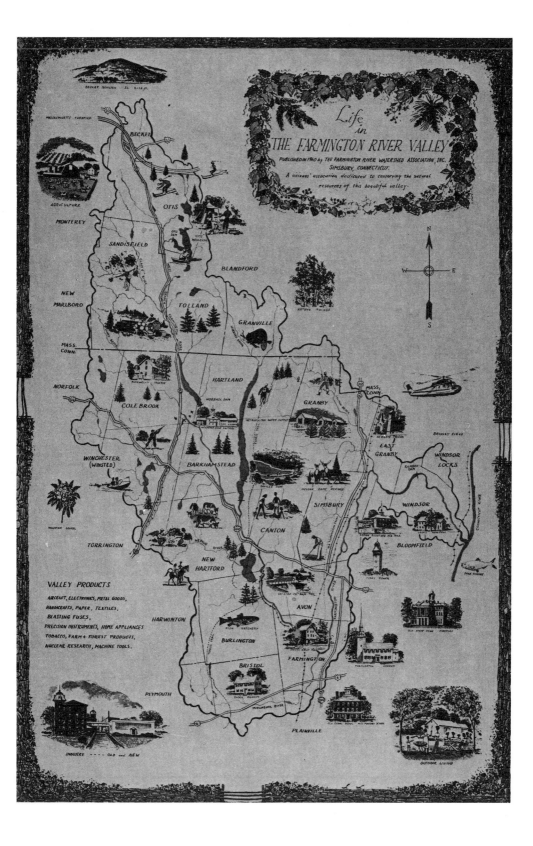

Preface

Throughout most of my life I have been intrigued by the people and events that have made Connecticut history. Review of many historical documents, tales told by old timers, and recollections of my youth have been woven into the fabric from which this volume is fashioned. It is designed to give some intimate glimpses of Connecticut's past, its people and its progress.

Some years ago I wrote a series of newspaper articles about the history of the Farmington River Valley. In 1960 I worked with Canton teachers to produce a history of the Town of Canton and a simple Connecticut history for use in the local elementary schools.

Since that time I have frequently visited both public and private elementary schools to help bring history to life with stories and slides. Children's responses to these visits have convinced me of the need for giving young people an understanding of the present through familiarity with the past.

More recently I met with Ruth D. Maher, primary grade teacher of Cherry Brook School in Canton Center, and Dr. H. B. Jestin, Vice President for Academic Affairs at Central Connecticut State College, to plan a series of stories about Connecticut that could be used in schools. Most of our work was done around a kitchen table. The stories were written for young people. Dr. Jestin and Mrs. Maher assisted in providing materials and in writing and editing. The illustrations are from my collection of works by R.J. Holden.

These are simply stories regarding Connecticut life from its beginnings to the contemporary scene. It is our hope that they please young and old alike.

1980   L. K. Porritt

Introduction

Mr. L. K. Porritt did much to increase knowledge and appreciation of our historical background. Local school programs were greatly enriched by his contributions. He wrote textbooks dealing with town and state history for use in the early elementary grades. He supplemented the written material with classroom visits to show exquisite slides from his personal collection or to discuss with students various phases of state or local history. Because of his willingness to share his enormous talents, young people continue to develop an increasing awareness of our history. In his efforts to inspire genuine appreciation of our heritage, Mr. Porritt himself has become a part of that heritage.

Stories of Connecticut presents a very readable and interesting history of Connecticut's growth from the glacial period through early aspects of its commercial and industrial development. The stories deal with the cause and effect relationships of historical personalities and events. The reader will gain understanding of many facets of Connecticut's cultural, economic, educational, industrial and legislative foundations. The book emphasizes the importance of individual ideas and accomplishments that led to the establishment of Connecticut as a strong, stable "Land of Steady Habits." Our work with Mr. Porritt has been a source of great inspiration and satisfaction. We are grateful for the assistance and cooperation of the Farmington Public Library, Louis Ball of the Farmington Valley Herald and Jane Goedecke of the Canton Historical Museum.

Unhappily, Mr. Porritt died in 1982, but his spirit is very much with us through these stories.

H. B. Jestin

Ruth Maher

CONTENTS

Illustrations

Chapter One

How The Glacier Changed The Face Of Connecticut

If we could have visited Connecticut 25,000 years ago, we would have found it very difficult to keep warm or to find any food to eat. On the other hand, we could have gone sliding or skating during any month of the year for there was little to be seen but ice. At that time a huge glacier covered all New England. The glacier was a moving mountain of ice, more than a mile thick in many places. It pushed its way down from the north through Vermont, New Hampshire and Massachusetts across Connecticut. Like a giant bulldozer, it scraped off the tops of mountains, uprooted great trees and pushed huge boulders as if they were pebbles. The glacier moved very slowly, probably not more than half a mile each year. But it was so big nothing could stop it.

No one knows for certain what caused this huge mountain of ice to form far south of the Arctic Circle. One guess is that the sea level was higher than it is today. This made it possible for the Gulf Stream to flow into the Arctic Ocean and warm the water enough to keep it free from ice all through the year. The cold dry winds, which constantly sweep out of the north, picked up tons of moisture while blowing across the great body of open water. When these northwest winds swept over Canada, they dropped huge quantities of moisture in the form of snow.

Each winter brought so much snow that only part of it melted during the following summer. Gradually the field of snow, which covered hundreds of thousands of square miles, became deeper and deeper. The weight of top layers packed bottom layers into ice. After thousands of years the ice formed an immense glacier which began to slide southward. Slowly the glacier moved across the northeastern part of the United States, snapping trees like matchsticks, scooping out great holes which became lakes, changing mountains and carving out valleys, bulldozing its way steadily to the sea.

Before the glacier moved across Connecticut, the Farmington River flowed almost straight south from its source in Massachusetts to New Haven, where it entered the sea. The glacier deposited a high ridge of gravel across the river bed of the Farmington between Plainville and Southington. When the glacier moved on and the river began to flow again, this ridge acted as a dam which prevented the river from following its old course to the sea at New Haven. The water held back by this dam formed a huge lake which covered the land now known as the towns of Plainville, Farmington, Canton, Avon, Simsbury and Granby.

Finally, the level of the water rose so high that it broke through the mountain at Tariffville. Gradually the rushing water cut a new path through the rock and earth. Now the Farmington River flows south to Unionville, east to Farmington, north to Tariffville, and east to Windsor. At Windsor it joins the Connecticut River on its way to the sea.

Before the glacier changed the face of Connecticut, some of our mountains were probably a mile or more in height. The glacier ground them down so that today Connecticut's highest mountains, Mount Frissell, Bear Mountain in Salisbury and Balk Hill in Union are less than half a mile high.

A map will help us understand how powerful the glacier was, and how much earth it pushed ahead of it. When the glacier reached the Atlantic Ocean and the salt water melted the ice, the huge loads of earth dumped into the ocean formed Long Island, Plum Island, Fishers Island, Cape Cod, Nantucket, and Martha's Vineyard.

As the glacier scraped the tops off our highest mountains, it ground the great masses of rock into millions of boulders and smaller stones. Not all of the gravel and earth was pushed as far as the sea. Millions of stones were scattered over Connecticut fields and hillsides, many of which were used to build the picturesque stone walls we see today. Some big piles of gravel fell aside as the glacier moved along. These are called *drumlins*, *eskers*, or *moraines*, depending on their form or shape. If you live in central Connecticut and would like to see one of these glacial deposits, there is a very interesting one on the east side of Tillotson Road in Avon. Tillotson Road runs between Avon and Farmington, just west of the Farmington River. This pile of glacial drift is long and smoothly rounded at the ends. It rises from the flat meadow like the back of a huge whale rising above the surface of the ocean.

There is no danger that another glacier may pass over New England during our lifetime. The Arctic Ocean is covered with ice, and the winds that sweep across it pick up little moisture. Most of the snow that falls on our country melts in the spring and does not build up layers of ice year after year.

Connecticut has changed greatly since the last ice of the glacier melted away. It has become a region of pleasant rivers, woodland lakes, green fields, rolling hills, and small mountains. Most towns in the state are within an hour's drive of the beaches along the shore of Long Island Sound. Although our weather changes with the seasons, we seldom suffer extreme heat or cold. Many people believe Connecticut is a wonderful state in which to live.

Chapter Two

The Indians of Connecticut (Upon The Long River)

No one knows how many Indians were living in Connecticut when the first European explorers visited the region. The Indians of New England left no written records; they had neither an alphabet nor a number system. They barely scratched the surface of the land on which they lived. When a village was moved or destroyed, the Indians left no cellar holes, chimneys, paved roads, or stone bridges as clues to the number of people who had lived there. Men who have spent years studying the Indians think there were not more than five thousand Indians in Connecticut when the first white men came.

Indian villages were quite different from our towns and cities. The homes were made of skins and bark rather than wood, brick, or stone. There were no churches, schools, stores, or factories. The children learned to fish, hunt, plant corn, cure skins, and preserve foods by helping their parents with these tasks.

The Indians had no sheep, cows, or other domesticated animals except, perhaps, dogs. They did not know how to raise cotton or flax, and they had not learned to spin thread from plant or animal fibers. Having no thread or yarn, they could not weave cloth. Animal skins supplied the material for their clothing.

They did not know that metals such as iron, copper, lead, and gold were hidden in certain kinds of rocks. They had not learned that people in other parts of the world knew how to get such metals out of the rocks by putting the ore into very hot fires and then shaping or casting the hot metal into knives, axes, kettles, and other tools and utensils. The Connecticut Indians made their weapons and tools of stone. Hatchets, knives, spearheads, and arrowheads were made by chipping stone to a sharp edge. Wooden handles were tied on with thongs cut from animal skins. Smaller tools, such as needles, were sometimes made of bone. Their hunting weapons were bows and arrows, for they did not know how to make guns and gunpowder. They boiled food by placing it in a hollowed out wood or stone pot and dropping very hot stones into it.

Europeans knew how to build sailing ships in which they were able to cross the ocean, but the Indians had never discovered that a sail could make it possible to capture the power of the wind. When they traveled by water, they had to depend on their own muscle power to move their paddles. For traveling by land the Indians had no carts or wagons. They had never heard of the wheel.

The Indians had no coins or paper money. They used beaver skins, wampum, and arrowheads for money. Wampum was made of small pieces of colored shells. Holes were drilled through the shells to form beads, which were strung in patterns and designs on strings of bark or leather.

Even though there were many things the Indians had not discovered, they knew all about nearly every plant that grew in the forest, field, or swamp. They knew which plants

3

Indians spearing fish at the rapids

had leaves, roots, bark, berries, or seeds that were good for food, and they knew which plants could be used for medicines. Although the compass and the clock were unknown to them, the Indians had learned that the sun, moon, and stars could help them find directions, predict the weather, and measure the passing of time and the changing seasons.

There was a good reason why the Connecticut Indians established their villages on the larger rivers and along the shore. Deer, foxes, rabbits, birds, other small animals, and a few bears and wild turkeys could be found in Connecticut woodlands. But there were no great herds of big game such as the buffalo herds that roamed the plains to the west. If the Indians had had to depend on their bows and arrows to provide food, often they would have gone hungry.

There was a more plentiful food supply in the rivers. Each spring millions of salmon, shad, sturgeon, lamprey eels, alewives and other fish would leave the ocean and swim far up the rivers to spawn in fresh water. The rivers were so full of fish that the Indians found it easier to get their food by fishing than by hunting. Without metal for hooks or thread for lines and nets, they could not fish as we do. They used spears with sharp stone spearheads.

The Indians knew it was difficult to spear fish where the water was deep, because the handles of their spears were not long enough to reach bottom. They knew, too, that where there was little current and the water was smooth, a man's shadow could scare away the fish. They had learned that the best place to spear fish was at the falls or rapids where the current was swift and the water shallow. There the fish swam more slowly against the swift current, and often they broke the surface of the water as they tried to jump the falls. There the fishermen could wade out to the middle of the river where the swift, broken water prevented their shadows from scaring the fish. Even the children were able to spear fish. Some of the best places to spear salmon, shad or lamprey eels were at the rapids or falls of the Farmington or Housatonic Rivers. Where the Farmington River breaks through the mountains at Tariffville, there was a series of falls and rapids. Because of the good places to spear fish, a settlement of Massacoe Indians grew up there.

During the spring and summer the river Indians were very busy with their fishing spears. A large supply of fish had to be smoked and stored away for the winter. In order to be near their main source of food, the Indians set up their villages close to the falls and swift rapids in Connecticut rivers. Many of the towns which later grew up along the rivers were located near the same falls and rapids, for the early settlers needed swiftly moving water to provide power for the mills where they sawed lumber, ground grain, or made gunpowder.

Probably two-thirds of the Connecticut Indians lived along the shore. These Indians could not fish with spears, because there were no rapids or falls where the rivers flowed into the sea. The shore tribes dug clams, raked oysters, trapped crabs and lobsters, and sometimes caught a few salt water fish. Clams, mussels, oysters and other shellfish could be found all through the year. The salt water and the rising and falling tides prevent ice from covering the sea as it often covers the rivers. Having a plentiful food supply always at hand, the Indian villages along the shore were larger than those on the rivers.

The Pequots were not one of the Connecticut fishing tribes. They were a warlike hunting tribe who had moved from northern New York to Connecticut several years before the first European settlers arrived. As they migrated southeastward through Connecticut, the Pequots conquered or killed all other tribes in their path. If there had been any Indians in the northwest corner of Connecticut before the Pequot migration, the Pequots killed them or drove them away. Early explorers found no Indians in the Housatonic valley above New Milford. The Pequots finally settled on the Thames River. They continued to fight and conquer other tribes, from whom they collected tribute.

The Pequots were the only Connecticut Indians who caused the early settlers any great trouble. After the English had begun to establish settlements in Connecticut, a number of Pequot warriors were murdered by some renegades from the Massachusetts Bay Colony. In revenge the Pequots raided the Wethersfield settlement, killing three women and six men, and taking two women as prisoners. Hartford, Windsor, and Wethersfield sent a company of soldiers under the command of Captain John Mason to avenge the Wethersfield raid. Captain Mason's men surrounded the Pequot village in Mystic, set it afire, and shot all the Pequots who tried to flee from the flames. The remaining Pequots were afraid to attack any English settlement, and a short time later they moved back to New York.

West of the Hudson River in New York lived the Mohawks, a tribe of fierce fighters who were feared by all the Indians of New England. In the Mohawk lands there were no big rivers full of sea-run fish. A Mohawk had to use his bow and arrow every day hunting for bears, deer, or smaller game. He became highly skilled in the use of the bow and arrow, which was the Indian weapon of war.

Before the Europeans came to Connecticut, a band of Mohawks had come down from the northwest and conquered the Tunxis, the Massacoes, the Poquonnocs and the other river Indians who lived west of the Connecticut River. To each tribe they had conquered the Mohawks said, "You must pay us beaver skins and strings of wampum. Each year we will send messengers to collect this tribute. If you do not pay, we will send a great war party to destroy your village."

The fishing tribes did not like to pay tribute to the Mohawks and the Pequots. They needed all their skins and wampum for their own use, but they knew that if they refused to pay, their enemies would destroy them. Year after year they handed over beaver skins and wampum to the Mohawk or Pequot messengers, hoping all the time that someone would come and help set them free.

While this was going on in Connecticut, the English had built settlements on the shore of Massachusetts Bay. The chief of one of the river tribes heard about the strange white people and their deadly guns. He talked with the leaders of other fishing tribes. "At last," he said, "here are people who can set us free. These white men, with their guns, are stronger than our conquerors. They will help us win the fight against our enemies. We will no longer have to pay tribute every year. Let us invite these white people to come and live among us. Let us share our lands with them; we will show them how to fish in our rivers and hunt in our forests. Let us welcome them as friends."

The river tribes sent messengers to Massachusetts Bay. They invited the English to come and look over Connecticut's fertile fields and rivers filled with fish. The people on the shores of Massachusetts Bay were already beginning to feel crowded, and still more people kept arriving from England. The Massachusetts Bay settlers knew the Dutch had built the House of Good Hope in Hartford, and they were afraid that the Dutch would soon claim the whole Connecticut River valley. They decided to send scouts to Connecticut.

The English scouts were pleased with the green meadows and good soil they found in the river valleys of Connecticut. They were pleased by the friendly manner of the fishing Indians. They welcomed the promise that the Indians would sell them land. In England, when a man bought land, he paid money for it and received a paper that proved his ownership. They wanted to do the same thing in Connecticut. They wanted to pay for their land with clothes, blankets, cooking utensils, knives, and other things which the Indians considered more valuable than money. Most of all they wanted a paper to prove that they had paid for the land and it was theirs. Then no one else could claim their land after they had cut trees, cleared fields, built homes, and planted gardens.

There were several reasons why the English liked the idea of building their homes near the villages of the friendly river Indians. Many of the early settlers had been townspeople before leaving England. They knew little about rivers and forests. They could learn from the Indians how to catch fish and trap wild animals. The Indians would show them which plants were good for food and which could be used in making medicines. The English people knew all about the herbs and other plants that grew in England, but they found few familiar ones in this new land.

Friendly Indian neighbors were important to the settlers in another way. The settlers knew there was always danger of attack by the Pequots, Mohawks, and the Hurons, a fierce tribe from Quebec. The river Indians had scouts watching the trails by which enemy tribes might invade their lands. If danger threatened, they would warn their English friends to prepare to fight the invaders. White settlers who had no Indian friends often had no warning of danger until war whoops were ringing in their ears and blazing arrows were landing on their rooftops.

The English scouts reported that Connecticut land was fertile and the Indians were friendly. Some of the people in Massachusetts Bay decided to come to Connecticut, and soon the first English settlements were being established.

Captain Adrian Block sailing the Onrust up the Connecticut River, 1614

Chapter Three

White Settlers: First The Dutch – Then The English

The scouts from the Massachusetts Bay Colony were not the first white men to visit Connecticut. Several years earlier, Dutch explorers had established a colony on Manhattan Island, which they called New Amsterdam. Today the same place is called New York City. In 1613 one of the Dutch ships anchored in New York was destroyed by fire. The ship's sailors and captain, Adrian Block, cut down trees, sawed them into planks and built another vessel, using the nails and other metal fittings they removed from the hulk of their burned ship. They worked all winter to build the new ship. They named it Onrust, which means restless. It was one of the first ships built in America.

In 1614 Captain Block sailed his new ship into Long Island Sound, which he thought was a large bay. He sailed along the shores until he came to the mouth of a river. He went up the river to a point about halfway between Hartford and Windsor, about fifty miles from the Sound. As he explored the Connecticut River, Captain Block saw fertile fields, great forests, plenty of fish and game, and several Indian villages. Some of the Indians paddled their canoes out on the river to look at the Onrust. Never before had they seen a sailing ship moved by wind power instead of paddles. To them it seemed a kind of magic.

The Indians told Captain Block they would be happy to have the Dutch establish a trading post where they could trade furs for guns, iron pots, blankets, and other things they could not make. Captain Block spent some time trading with the Indians. Then he sailed on up the Connecticut River beyond Hartford until he came to rapids which his ship could not pass. The Onrust sailed back to Long Island Sound, and Captain Block continued exploring the Connecticut shore. He discovered Block Island, which was named for him.

When the Onrust returned to New York, Captain Block reported that the Connecticut River would be a good place to establish a trading post. But nineteen long years passed before the Dutch finally bought a strip of land one mile long and one-third of a mile wide in the middle of what is now Hartford. For this land they paid the Indians twenty yards of cloth, six axes, six kettles, eighteen knives, one sword blade, one pair of shears, and some toys. Today that land is worth millions of dollars.

In June, 1633, the Dutch used that small strip of land to establish a trading post, which was protected by two small cannon. They named their little fort the House of Good Hope. In order that Indians of all tribes might trade at the House of Good Hope without fear of their enemies, weapons had to be left at the gate.

The chiefs of several Connecticut tribes had been trying for a long time to persuade the English people in Massachusetts to settle in Connecticut. When the English learned that the Dutch had built a trading post on the Connecticut River, they decided to find out

Thomas Hooker's band of settlers traveling from Cambridge to Hartford, 1636

more about Connecticut. Both the Dutch and the English wanted to claim as much of the new world as they could control.

In October, 1633, a small group of men from Plymouth Colony in Massachusetts came by boat to Hartford. The distance is almost twice as far by water as by land, but they could carry more winter supplies on a boat than they could carry on their backs if they walked. They even brought with them the frame of a hut. When the Plymouth people sailed past the House of Good Hope, the Dutch were angry. They ordered the English to turn back, but they did not fire their cannon. The Plymouth people sailed on until they reached the place where the Farmington River flows into the Connecticut River at Windsor. They bought some land from the Podunk Indians and set up their house.

The Pequots were angry when they learned that the English had paid the Podunks for land that had been conquered by the Pequots. This may have been one of the reasons why the Pequots later raided Wethersfield.

In the fall of 1634 John Oldham and a little company of men from Massachusetts Bay walked through the forests to a place called Pyquag, which is now Wethersfield. They built crude huts to shelter them from the cold weather, but they had not been able to carry enough food to last through the winter. If the Indians had not been kind enough to give them food, these brave men might have died before spring.

In May, 1636, Thomas Hooker led a group of people from Cambridge in Massachusetts to Hartford. There were no roads between Cambridge and Hartford. Thomas Hooker's group followed Indian trails, which were too rough and narrow for wagons. Everything they took with them was carried on their backs. It must have looked like a long parade as they walked single file through the woods and fields. But one of them later said they had no marching music except the lowing of their cattle and the squealing of their pigs. It took Hooker and his followers about a month to go from Cambridge to Hartford. Mrs. Hooker was so ill that she had to be carried in a sling much of the way. It was a difficult trip, and the travelers were happy to arrive at the banks of the beautiful Connecticut River.

Originally, Hartford was called New Towne, and neighboring settlements were known as Watertown and Dorchester. Because several members of the colony had come from Hertford, England, New Towne was renamed Hartford. During the same period, Watertown became Wethersfield and the settlers at Dorchester changed the name of their colony to Windsor.

Many other English settlers soon came to Connecticut, and in 1654 the Dutch became discouraged and left their House of Good Hope to go back to New York. A few years after the founding of Hartford, New Haven was settled under the leadership of Theophilus Eaton and the Reverend John Davenport, who had come directly from England. The people of New Haven disagreed with some of Hartford's ideas. They wanted to remain separate from all other New England colonies, but when King Charles II granted Connecticut's charter, New Haven was included as part of the Connecticut Colony.

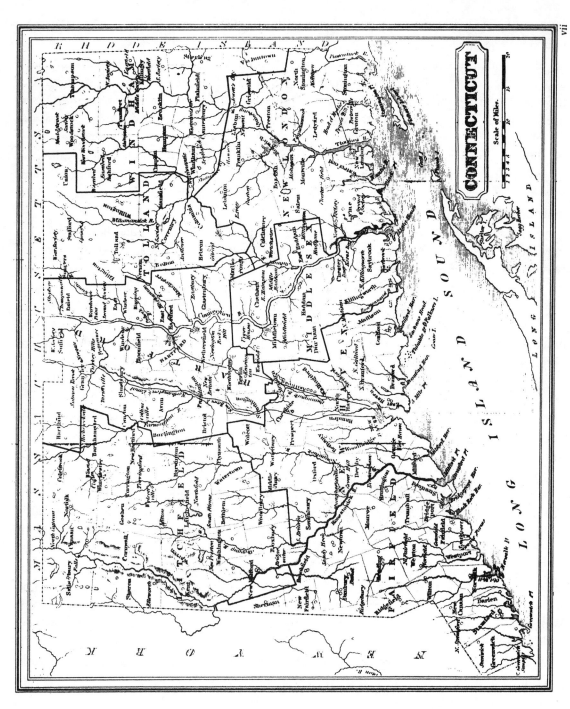

Map of present day Connecticut

Chapter Four

Connecticut's Charter

For the first year or two of their existence Hartford, Windsor, and Wethersfield regarded themselves as part of the Massachusetts colony. But when the governor of Massachusetts was called upon to send soldiers and raise money to help the Connecticut settlements fight the Pequots, he gave no answer. It was nearly a hundred miles from the Pequot fort in Mystic to Boston or Cambridge. The governor felt sure that the Pequots would not walk that far to attack the Massachusetts Bay towns. In 1637 the three Connecticut settlements declared themselves independent of Massachusetts. As soon as they had disposed of the Pequots, they began to make plans for organizing their own government.

Thomas Hooker firmly believed that the people of the Connecticut colony should govern themselves. He felt that they had the right to choose the men who would rule the colony and to turn these men out of office if they did not do a good job. If he had expressed such ideas in England, the king might have thrown him into prison or cut off his head. At that time the English king believed whatever he did or said was absolutely right, even if his decisions were foolish or cruel. Many years passed before the English changed that belief, which was called the Divine Right of Kings.

In 1638 rules for governing the colony were written. They were based on Thomas Hooker's belief that government should be by consent of the governed. This set of rules was called the Fundamental Orders. It was the first step toward the Declaration of Independence, which was written about one hundred forty years later.

The Fundamental Orders did not solve all the problems that worried the leaders of the Connecticut colony. The boundaries of the colony were not clearly defined. In 1644 George Fenwick ceded to the Connecticut colony hundreds of square miles of land he had been granted at the mouth of the Connecticut River. Unfortunately, he was unable to show any deed to prove his ownership. Therefore, Connecticut had no proof of its right to claim the land. New Haven colony was also a problem. Hartford firmly believed that New Haven should be a part of Connecticut, even if the New Haven colonists disagreed. Also, the Connecticut leaders had not told the English king how they were running the colony under the Fundamental Orders. They wanted to tell him about it in their own way, rather than to have him hear the news from someone else. It must be tactfully explained, or the king might even consider it treason.

After Charles II had been made king, it was decided to draw up a charter that would clearly define the boundaries of the colony, include New Haven as a part of Connecticut, and grant the king's permission to run the colony as the leaders had been running it under the Fundamental Orders. Getting the king to sign this paper was something that could not be done by mail. If the king were not in the right mood when asked to sign the charter, or if he decided to read it carefully before attaching the royal seal, Connecticut's days as an independent colony might end just as they were about to begin.

Most people agreed that Governor John Winthrop was the right man to go to London and try to secure the kind of charter the colony wanted. He came from a highly respected English family. He was well educated. Perhaps most important, he had several friends who were favorites of the king. The colony granted him 500 English pounds (about $2500) for expenses.

He planned to sail from New Amsterdam (now New York) on July 20, 1661. On his boat trip from Hartford to New Amsterdam he was delayed by unfavorable winds and weather and did not arrive until after his ship was supposed to sail. The Dutch governor, Peter Stuyvesant, ordered the ship held in port until Governor Winthrop arrived. The Dutch governor's kindness to an Englishman was a pleasing contrast to the manner in which the English had treated the Dutch in Hartford.

Had Charles II known that New Haven was then hiding the three judges who had condemned his father to death, it would have been difficult for Governor Winthrop to gain any favors for Connecticut. Fortunately, the king did not learn about this until after Winthrop had pleaded his case.

Everything worked well for Governor Winthrop. His influential friends were able to arrange a meeting with the king under favorable conditions. Winthrop was a gentleman and a scholar, and Charles II could not help liking him. Winthrop outlined briefly what the Connecticut colony wished to include in the charter. The king told him to go ahead and draw up the document. Winthrop had two copies made, and the king gave the charter his royal approval.

The colonists of Connecticut were pleased when Governor Winthrop returned with the charter. Now they had the king's permission to run their colony as they had been running it under the Fundamental Orders. The boundaries were clearly defined. All doubts about ownership of the Fenwick lands were laid to rest, and New Haven was made part of the Connecticut colony. New Haven did not like this. What New Haven wanted most was to be left alone. Hartford wisely avoided interfering with the way New Haven managed its affairs, and few troubles arose between them.

The colonists were so pleased with the good job Governor Winthrop had done that they set about raising the 500 English pounds they had promised him. Few people had money in those days, so they paid their share in bushels of peas and wheat. Hartford's share was one-fourth of the total amount. Hartford paid Governor Winthrop 500 bushels of wheat and 300 bushels of peas.

Things progressed smoothly for about twenty-five years, although there was some trouble with the Indians during this period. An Indian chief named King Philip rallied the remnants of several tribes and made one last attempt to drive out the settlers. By that time King Philip's men had guns which made them far more dangerous than the Pequots with their bows and arrows. But most of the raids were against Massachusetts settlements. Except for the destruction of Simsbury, which was burned after its people had fled back to Windsor, Connecticut did not suffer greatly. On most occasions Connecticut dealt wisely with the Indians and did not anger them with foolish laws as some other colonies did.

Charles II died in 1685, and James II became king of England. One of King James' favorites was Sir Edmund Andros. He persuaded the king that all the New England colonies should be united under one governor and hinted that he would be a good governor. King James agreed and gave Andros a royal commission as Governor of New England.

This was bad news for the Connecticut colony. Connecticut had had dealings with Sir Edmund Andros when he was governor of New York. Andros had tried to claim that the Connecticut River was the eastern boundary of New York. He came to Saybrook with a small company of soldiers to take over the southwestern part of Connecticut. Fortunately, Connecticut had a larger company of soldiers there under the command of Thomas Bull. When Andros announced that he had come to accept the surrender of the Saybrook fort and this section of Connecticut, Bull laughed at him. He told Andros it might be wise for him to get back to New York in a hurry. Otherwise, Bull hinted, his men might find it necessary to do a little shooting. Andros saw that he was outnumbered and if there were a fight he would almost certainly be killed. He followed Thomas Bull's advice, but he was very angry with Connecticut. For the next few years he waited for an opportunity for revenge.

His chance came when James II became king of England. One of the reasons why Andros wanted to become Governor of New England was that Connecticut would then be placed under his power and could be punished for the humiliation its soldiers had inflicted on him at Saybrook.

As soon as he had settled in Boston, Andros wrote a letter to Connecticut's Governor Treat. He told the governor that he was coming to Hartford to take back the charter which gave Connecticut the right to rule its colony according to the Fundamental Orders. This was in December, 1686.

But Sir Edmund made a serious mistake. He waited about ten months before coming to pick up the charter. That gave the leaders of the Connecticut colony plenty of time to make plans for outwitting him. On one thing these men were in full agreement. Not one of them was willing to surrender the charter to Andros. If he took it by force, that would be something they could not prevent. But they would not hand over the charter without a struggle.

On October 26, 1687, Andros made his long expected visit. Hartford was about fifty years old and had about 1200 inhabitants. Andros and his company of soldiers and aides spent the night of October 25 at Norwich. On horseback they rode from Norwich to Wethersfield, were ferried across the river, and rode into Hartford on the evening of October 26. Hartford's reception was cool but correct. No one cheered and no one jeered. Hartford had no love for Andros, but he was the agent of the King of England, and it was wise to treat him with restraint if not respect.

A meeting was quickly arranged between Andros, his aides, and several leaders of the colony. They sat around a large table in one of Hartford's taverns. The charter was brought in and laid on the table. As it grew dark, candles were lighted.

Suddenly the candles were blown out. There were no matches in those days, and it took a minute or two to get a light from the fire. When the candles were relighted, the charter had vanished. No one seemed to know what had happened to it. That ended the meeting, and the next morning Andros left for Boston, burning with anger at the people of Hartford.

It was not by accident that those candles went out. It had all been carefully planned before Andros came to Hartford. Someone was to wait in the darkness behind the tavern, under the window of the meeting room. When the candles were blown out, one of the men in the room was to lift the charter from the table and quietly slip it through the window to the man who was waiting below. He was to hide it in a safe place, but not in a house. Andros might order that every house in town be searched. It might have meant death to any man in whose home the charter was found. The hiding place was well chosen. Legend tells us the charter was hidden in a hollow oak, long since known as the Charter Oak.

Before Andros was able to devise some new way of getting revenge against Connecticut, James II resigned as king. The English people had grown tired of him. They told him to get out of England and stay out. His daughter Mary and her husband William were invited to become queen and king. They were known as William and Mary because they shared the job of ruling England. William and Mary did not like Sir Edmund Andros. They told him he was through as Governor of New England and ordered him to take the first ship back to England. Connecticut quietly brought its charter out of hiding. The leaders began again to run the colony as they had been doing before Andros tried to interfere.

The Fundamental Orders and the Connecticut charter were very important papers. They were the first steps taken by any of the American colonies toward self-rule by freeing themselves from interference by the English king. The Declaration of Independence and the Constitution of the United States were both influenced by these documents which Connecticut had drawn up more than a hundred years before.

Chapter Five

Life In Early Connecticut

A long time ago a small trunk, filled with letters and papers, was hidden away in the attic of an old house in Canton. For many years the trunk was forgotten. It lay untouched by anyone except the mice and squirrels that chewed holes in some of the papers as they gathered materials for their nests.

One day the little trunk was finally found and opened. Its contents told a fascinating story of how people lived and earned their living in the latter half of the eighteenth century.

Like a bright thread running through a piece of plain cloth, the story of Dr. Solomon Everest, who lived from approximately 1750 to 1810, was woven through this assortment of old letters and papers. Dr. Everest happened to live in Canton, but his way of life would have been much the same if he had lived in any one of a score of other small towns in the state.

Dr. Everest lived in a beautiful old house which still stands at the corner of Albany Turnpike and Lawton Road in Canton. He had few of the conveniences we take for granted today. Television, radio and the telephone were unknown. There were no electric lights. Dr. Everest lighted his home with tallow candles made from the fat of animals that had been butchered for meat.

All the water for cooking, drinking, bathing and laundry had to be carried in a bucket from the well. Dr. Everest's well was close to the back door, but many families had to carry water a long way from springs or streams.

Most of Dr. Everest's fruits and vegetables came from his own garden. He had several cows which provided milk, butter and cheese. But, because he was busy taking care of his patients, there were many things he could not make or grow for his family. He did not have time to raise flax and wool to be spun into thread or yarn and woven into cloth. He was too busy to cut and store all the wood needed for the huge fireplaces that provided heat to warm his home and cook his food.

There were no oil burners in those days, and people did not know there was plenty of coal in the mountains of Pennsylvania. Even if they had known about the coal, there were no railroads or canals over which the coal could have been transported to Connecticut. In Norwich, Middletown, Stamford and other towns near shipping ports some people had stoves in which they burned coal. They could buy the coal from English ships, which sometimes carried many tons of it as ballast.

Even if Dr. Everest had been able to buy coal in nearby Hartford, it was not until about 1800 that it became possible to haul heavy loads, such as coal or iron stoves, to Canton. After the Revolution, Franklin stoves could be bought in towns such as New London, Essex and Milford, where they could be brought by boat from the foundry in

New Jersey. But Dr. Everest could not enjoy the warmth and convenience of a stove until the opening of the Albany Turnpike made it possible to haul a heavily loaded wagon over the mountain from Hartford.

In Dr. Everest's time winter was something to be feared. There were no snowplows to keep the roads open. When a family was snowed in by a bad storm, a week might pass before they could travel to the home of their nearest neighbor. Each family had to have plenty of salt pork, corn meal, potatoes and turnips stored in the cellar, or they might run out of food before spring. People had not yet learned that they could preserve fruits and vegetables, and even meats, by canning them or keeping them frozen. Long before spring the children must have grown tired of their winter diet. It is not surprising that when warm weather came, they were eager to search the meadows for marsh marigolds, fern fiddles and other edible greens.

Dr. Everest's father was a doctor who had learned from the Indians which plants and berries would help cure sick people. When Solomon Everest decided to become a doctor, he did not go to medical school. He rode around with his father, who showed him how to find herbs and taught him all he could about treating patients.

When illness struck a family, someone would have to run to the doctor's home and tell him he was needed. Of course Dr. Everest had no automobile. During his first years as a doctor he rode horseback to answer his calls. Later, when roads were made smoother and wider, he used a carriage.

Small Connecticut towns had no drug stores from which doctors could order medicines. Often, on his way to visit a sick person, Dr. Everest would stop his horse and walk into the woods to look for the roots, bark, leaves or berries which might cure the patient he had been called to treat.

Dr. Everest was rarely paid money for his services. There was very little silver money in Connecticut before the Revolution. Connecticut had no rich gold or silver mines. Money brought in from trade with the West Indies was used to pay for manufactured products that had to be bought from England. Paper money had not yet come into use, and many Connecticut farmers saw no silver coins from one year to the next. They raised or made almost everything they needed. Their surplus farm products were traded for the things they could not provide themselves. Such products were also used as payment for the services of the minister, the doctor, the miller and the blacksmith.

One local family kept a large flock of sheep. The women of the household used their wool to make beautiful homespun cloth. They produced more than the family needed in order that the surplus might be used to pay for things they could not make. One year they owed Dr. Everest eight dollars for sixteen visits he had made during the winter. They paid him eight yards of sturdy homespun cloth, enough to make him a fine new suit.

Another of Dr. Everest's patients raised large fields of flax. The flax fibers were spun, woven and bleached to make beautiful white linen. This family paid the doctor with yards of linen, from which Mrs. Everest made shirts and sheets. Another patient paid his bill with leather he had tanned himself. When the traveling shoemaker stayed a couple of weeks at the Everest home, he used the leather to make shoes for the whole family. Several patients paid Dr. Everest with cords of wood already cut in fireplace lengths.

In those days doctors did not know that people could be vaccinated against such dreaded diseases as smallpox, typhoid and diphtheria. Sometimes diphtheria would kill three or four children in the same family within one week. About one of every three people who caught smallpox died.

Some Farmington doctors learned that people usually recovered from smallpox if they caught it in the winter and were given good food and care. These doctors opened a hospital on Rattlesnake Mountain. Groups of boys and girls were taken there in the winter to be given smallpox. They had to stay at the hospital until they got well, but none of them died. The Farmington hospital was called Hospital Rock. There was a big flat rock in front of it, where people who were getting well would lie in the sun and sometimes carve their initials in the soft stone. Patients at the hospital could be visited by other people who had already had smallpox. Anyone who had recovered from the disease was not likely to catch it again. Probably Dr. Everest and many others were greatly interested in the Hospital Rock experiment. In 1796 Dr. Edmund Jenner, an English physician, discovered that an injection of a very mild disease called cowpox would prevent the more deadly smallpox. This was the beginning of vaccination and other medical findings which have since saved millions of lives.

American soldiers during the Revolutionary War

Chapter Six

Trouble With England – Then Revolution

If England's King George III had been a wiser man, war between England and the colonies might have been avoided. The United States might have gained its independence by peaceful steps as Canada has done.

Many colonists believed it was only fair that the American colonies should pay part of the cost of the French and Indian wars. As long as France held Canada, the French and their Indian allies were a constant threat to the New England colonies. But, instead of talking it over with the leaders of the colonies and working out a plan that would be agreeable to both, the English said, "You must buy stamps and put them on all your important papers. You must also pay a duty on all the tea you import."

The American colonies had to pay these taxes, but they were allowed no part in passing the laws that levied them. This is what is meant by taxation without representation.

There was something else that angered many Connecticut people even more than taxation without representation. England looked upon her American colonies as a source of raw materials and a market for English goods. She would not let the colonists start any business that might interfere with any English business. Right here in Connecticut was a good example. Copper was discovered at East Granby. The English allowed the colonists to mine the copper ore. But they said, "You may not smelt that ore. You must send it to England to be smelted and made into such products as bowls, frying pans, and hinges. Then you may buy these things from English factories."

If that copper ore could have been smelted in Connecticut, and if the pans and hinges could have been manufactured here, it would have helped Connecticut in two ways. It would have provided jobs for many Connecticut people. The finished products would have been much less expensive for Connecticut people, because the cost of the round trip across the Atlantic would have been eliminated. But the English did not care about jobs for the colonists. They were more interested in jobs for the people of England.

The first boatload of ore sank in an Atlantic storm. The owner of the mine went down with the ship. After his death no one else wanted to carry on the business, and the East Granby copper mine lay idle for many years.

Luckily for Connecticut, there was one industry which England did allow the colonists to establish. That was the smelting of iron ore. There was a good reason why the English allowed blast furnaces to be built here. Before people learned to use coke, it took many bushels of charcoal to smelt a ton of pig iron. Many trees were needed to make all this charcoal. England had no great forests like those in the colonies, and English iron furnaces had been using trees faster than new ones were growing. There was not enough wood left to keep the English people warm, to cook their food, and to make their floors and furniture. Laws had to be passed forbidding the starting of new furnaces and cutting down the use of existing ones.

But the English needed iron. When rich iron ore was discovered in Salisbury, Connecticut men were allowed to start a blast furnace. Probably the English would have insisted that the cast iron pigs be shipped to England to be made into useful things in their factories, but English soldiers fired on the colonial militia at Lexington before the Salisbury furnace began to pour its first iron. After that Connecticut people no longer allowed the English to tell them what they must do.

It was lucky for the colonists that the Salisbury furnace was ready to go to work when the Revolution started. There were few other blast furnaces in the colonies, and the American army needed cannon, muskets, bayonets, anchors and dozens of other things made of iron. Had it not been for the Salisbury furnace, it would have been much more difficult for General Washington to win the war.

The Salisbury furnace was owned by a man named Richard Smith. He was a Tory. Tories were loyal to the English king and did not want the colonies to declare their independence. Fearing for his safety, Smith left for England when the Revolutionary War started. Before he left, he turned over the furnace to Governor Jonathan Trumbull of Connecticut. After the war, he returned to Connecticut. Much to his surprise, Governor Trumbull gave him a large sum of money for all the iron made in his furnace during the war.

When war broke out between England and the American colonies, Governor Jonathan Trumbull of Connecticut was the only colonial governor who stuck to his job. All the others fled to England as fast as they could find ships to carry them. The governors of the other colonies had been appointed by the king, and they owed their loyalty to him. For more than a hundred years Connecticut had been operating under a charter which allowed the people of the colony to govern themselves. The people of Connecticut, through their representatives, had elected Jonathan Trumbull to be their governor. He owed his loyalty to these people rather than to the English king, and most Connecticut people wanted nothing more to do with the king. Therefore, Governor Trumbull stayed with the people who had chosen him when the other colonial governors fled back to the king who had appointed them.

Governor Trumbull was a good friend of General Washington. In fact, the general called him Brother Jonathan. When Washington came through Connecticut after taking command of the American army at Boston, he stopped to see his old friend.

"What can Connecticut do to help you win this war?" asked the governor. "Large numbers of our men are volunteering to serve in the army, but we want to do more. How can we help?"

"Brother Jonathan," the general replied, "if we are to win this war, my army will need just about all the supplies we can get. We will need wheat flour and corn meal for bread; cattle, sheep and hogs for meat; woolen cloth for uniforms and blankets; leather for shoes; horses to pull our cannon. We have money to pay for these things. Can you get them for us?"

"General, you have more than enough to do training your soldiers and leading them in battle," answered the Connecticut governor. "We people of Connecticut will see that your men have food and clothing." Jonathan Trumbull kept his word. He established his headquarters in a small building in the town of Lebanon where he lived. This building, called the War Office, still stands.

Governor Trumbull divided Connecticut into districts and appointed an agent for each district. "Visit every farm in your district," he told these men. "Buy all the corn, wheat, horses, cattle, hogs, sheep and homespun cloth that the farmers will sell. Pay them with this new paper money that Congress has ordered printed for this purpose, and tell them you will come back and buy more next year."

The agents visited every farm in their districts. They bought all the supplies that people could spare and paid for them with the new paper money. One farmer in Brooklyn had many yards of fine homespun cloth. He was planning to use it to make new clothes for the whole family. But when the agent told him that many of General Washington's soldiers had holes in their uniforms, he said, "Take it. Our soldiers need it more than we do."

Many Connecticut farmers were still living in the small crude shacks they had built when they first settled on their land. Many of these houses had dirt floors and no cellars. Most of them had a ladder leading to a loft instead of a staircase rising to nice upstairs bedrooms.

The dirt floors were very annoying to the women. No matter how hard they worked, the floors could not be swept clean. For years the women had wanted to build new and larger homes. They wanted cellars for storage. They wanted a big chimney in the middle of the house, with fireplaces on all sides to keep the house warmer in winter. But they had no money to hire masons and carpenters, and the men in the family had many other things to do in those early days. If the old house were strong enough to keep out the bears and wolves, and tight enough to keep out the rain and snow, that was good enough for the men. They were working outside all day; they did not have to sweep the dirt floors. As time went on, the women became more and more tired of their small crude houses. Sometimes they complained that the cows had a better home than the family.

Then Governor Trumbull's agents came riding through all the back roads of Connecticut towns, buying livestock, grain and clothing materials. For the first time in their lives, many farmers had large sums of money. For some of them, having money was such a new experience that they did not know what to do with it. There were no savings banks or investment stocks and bonds in those days.

"Abigail," a Connecticut farmer might have asked his wife, "what shall we do with all this money? If we keep it in the house, someone may steal it. If we hide it, the rats may eat it or the paper may get damp and moldy."

"You are right Ebenezer," Abigail might have answered. "Let us use it for something we need, something that will last a long time. Now you can hire skilled masons and carpenters instead of having to do all the work yourself. Let us build that new home we have been wanting for so many years."

The winter of 1777, when Washington's men were at Valley Forge, was long and bitterly cold. Food was very scarce. Many Pennsylvania farmers did not dare sell food to the colonial soldiers for fear of being punished by the British soldiers. Hundreds of cattle were driven from Connecticut to Valley Forge. Without the supplies from Connecticut, General Washington might have been unable to hold his army together through that terrible winter. With the money received for those supplies many Connecticut farm families paid for larger, more comfortable homes. Look at the dates on some of the beautiful old farmhouses that can be found in all parts of Connecticut. Notice that many were built during the years of the Revolution, between 1776 and 1784.

Chapter Seven

The Old North Road And The Battle of Saratoga

For more than a century after the first English colonists settled in Connecticut, little more than a series of Indian trails connected Hartford and Albany. There were no good roads anywhere in the Connecticut colony except the streets of some of the larger towns, and few of those were fit for wagons or carriages.

Derby, Essex, Milford and other towns that were on navigable rivers or had good harbors on Long Island Sound were able to have social and business relations with other towns on the river or coast. But inland towns such as Colchester, Litchfield, Hebron and Woodbury were like islands in a great sea of forest. Within each town, passable roads connected the various farms with the meetinghouse, gristmill and general store but the paths to neighboring towns were not much better than Indian trails. Such towns produced nearly everything they needed. They consumed nearly everything they produced. Simsbury, for example, had little to sell that Hartford or Farmington could not produce. As a consequence, Simsbury people had little money with which to buy those attractive imported articles brought into Hartford by boat. There was little need for anything more than an Indian trail from Farmington to Simsbury, and for more than a century a bridle path took care of the traffic between Simsbury and Hartford.

In 1754 the last of the French and Indian wars broke out. There was danger that the French might attack New England. There were two routes invading troops might take. They might go up the valley of the St. Francis and down the Connecticut River valley, or up the Richelieu, across Lake Champlain and Lake George, and down the Hudson River valley.

If the French came by way of the Connecticut River valley, troops from New York would have to be moved to the east to meet the invasion. If they came by the Hudson River valley, soldiers from Connecticut and Massachusetts would have to hurry to Albany to stop the invaders. But there was nothing more than an Indian trail through northwestern Connecticut. It was too rough and overgrown for soldiers on horseback, so the British army officers decided that a road must be built. They wanted it as short and straight as possible. It is said that the commanding officer took his map, a ruler and a pencil and drew a straight line between Weatogue on the Farmington River and Canaan on the Housatonic. (The only bridge across the upper Farmington River was at Weatogue. There was a bridle path between the bridge and Hartford.) Then he told the men who had been hired to build the road, "If you stray more than one mile from that line you will not be paid for your work."

As a result, this road, which was known as the Old North Road, ran over some of the highest mountain ridges and through some of the worst swamps in all of Connecticut. It ran through West Simsbury, North Canton, Barkhamsted, Colebrook and Norfolk. Some of the roughest parts were soon bypassed. About forty years later, sections of the Old North Road became part of the Albany Turnpike. The Old North Road was not smooth or wide enough for wagons or carriages. It was good only for men on horseback or soldiers on foot.

The French general, Montcalm, surrendered to General Wolfe at Quebec before he had a chance to try to invade New England. The last of the French and Indian wars ended before there was any need to use the Old North Road. But when the English found themselves at war with their American colonies, they decided to do what they had expected the French to do. They decided to invade New York and New England from Canada.

Lord Germain, the British Minister of War, worked out a clever plan. General Burgoyne was to come down from Canada by way of Lake Champlain and the upper Hudson River valley with 5000 hired Hessian soldiers. General Howe was to move up the Hudson from New York, bringing gunpowder and supplies. He was prepared to strike the rear of any colonial army that might be trying to stop Burgoyne. General St. Leger was to move down the Mohawk River valley and join the other two armies at Albany. The purpose was to cut off New England from the other colonies, crush the rebellion in New England, and then sweep down through the other colonies.

It was a well thought out plan. It might have worked except for one thing. General Howe did not receive his orders to move up the Hudson and meet Burgoyne. In London, Lord Germain had dictated the orders to be sent to the three generals. The orders to General Burgoyne and General St. Leger were clearly written and easy to read. He signed these and ordered that they be sent, but the orders to General Howe were badly written and blotted with ink. He was very angry about this and ordered that they be done over.

It was late in the day when the new set of orders for General Howe was ready. Lord Germain was in a hurry to leave his office. He was planning to leave London for the weekend. He said, "I haven't time to read and sign this now. Put it on my desk and I will do it first thing next week." Then he put on his hat and left. The orders to Howe were put on Lord Germain's desk. More papers came in. They were placed on top of the letter to Howe. Other papers were added to the pile. About six months later someone found Howe's orders.

Northwestern Vermont was very sparsely settled in 1777. There were few farms from which General Burgoyne could buy meat for his men. His soldiers had to shoot deer and other wild game for food. In trying to shoot game, the soldiers used much of their gunpowder and bullets. For a while this did not worry Burgoyne. He knew that Howe had been ordered to move up the Hudson to meet him and bring plenty of gunpowder before it would be needed.

But soon Burgoyne began to worry. His scouts told him that an American army was gathering near Saratoga to try to stop him, and that Howe was still in New York and showed no sign of getting ready to move. Burgoyne learned that the Americans had a storehouse full of gunpowder near Bennington. If he could capture this, it would solve his problem. He sent several hundred of his Hessian soldiers to Bennington with orders to seize the gunpowder. But Ethan Allen and his Green Mountain Boys wanted that gunpowder for their own use. They defeated the Hessians in a fierce fight. The surviving Hessians fled back to Burgoyne's army with a lot less gunpowder than they had when they started.

When General Washington learned that Burgoyne was marching down from Canada, he knew that Connecticut might be in for real trouble unless Burgoyne was stopped. He ordered Benedict Arnold to gather as many Connecticut soldiers as he could and to hurry over to Albany and try to stop Burgoyne.

Connecticut was very glad then that the Old North Road had been built. Those soldiers could not go from Hartford to Albany by boat because the British held New York and the lower Hudson. But they could march to Albany over the Old North Road in three or four days.

By this time, Burgoyne had plenty to worry him. Howe was still in New York, more than a hundred miles away. St. Leger was held up at Fort Stanwix and could not help. Burgoyne's soldiers had used up most of their gunpowder, and an American army had gathered near Saratoga to block his path.

The Americans fortified a ridge from which they could fire on anyone going down the Hudson valley by land or water. Burgoyne tried to capture this ridge but was thrown back. After his soldiers used up most of their small supply of gunpowder, they withdrew to a strongly fortified position.

Horatio Gates was the general in command of the Americans. Benedict Arnold, who had arrived with a large number of well trained soldiers from Connecticut, was second in command. Gates wanted to delay the attack on the British position until more men had arrived. Arnold knew that the British were short of gunpowder. He feared that if the Americans waited, Howe might come up the Hudson and attack them in the rear. He wanted to attack as soon as possible.

The story told is that Arnold said, "If you won't attack, I will," and he led his men against the strong British positions. Gates is said to have stayed in his tent all day, angry at Arnold for doing what he had been told not to do.

It was a hard fight. Both sides had many men killed or wounded. As long as their powder lasted, the Hessians fought bravely, but when it was all gone, they had to retreat. They fell back five or six miles to a village which they tried to fortify. Burgoyne knew that he was defeated. His troops were short of food as well as powder. His officers had used up all the wine and brandy they had brought from Canada. They had nothing to drink but homemade spruce beer, which they did not like. They, too, were ready to stop fighting.

When Gates heard that Burgoyne was ready to surrender, he forgot his quarrel with Arnold. He put on his best uniform and took charge of things. The terms he gave Burgoyne were very generous. If the officers promised not to fight the Americans again, they would not have to go to prison. They could stay with friends in the colonies until they were able to return to England. Some of them stayed in Farmington and Litchfield. The Hessian soldiers would be marched to Boston where ships would meet them and take them back to Germany.

The ships failed to arrive, and many of the Hessians went to live with other Germans in Pennsylvania. They became known as the Pennsylvania Dutch. Those Hessian prisoners who marched through Canaan, Norfolk, Colebrook and Canton were the only enemy soldiers that the people of these towns saw during all the years of the Revolution.

Many historians believe that Saratoga was the most important battle fought by American soldiers. Had they lost that battle, New England might have been overrun by the British, and General Washington might have lost the war.

But thanks to Lord Germain's carelessness, Arnold's grasp of Burgoyne's problems, and the bravery of colonial soldiers, the Americans won that battle. In winning they did more than capture thousands of prisoners. They defeated one of the best trained armies of Europe. This made the French king sit up and take notice and decide to send help to General Washington. It greatly cheered the fighting men in all the colonies, and caused many Tories to change their minds about being Tories.

Northern and central Connecticut suffered very little during the Revolution. People living in towns north of Danbury saw no enemy troops except prisoners of war, but towns within easy marching distance of the coast did not fare so well. In 1777, Tryon, the Royalist governor of New York, with twenty-five ships and two thousand men, landed at Saugatuck and marched on Danbury. He burned part of the town and destroyed supplies that had been stored there.

Benedict Arnold gathered all the soldiers he could find and attacked Tryon at Ridgefield while he was retreating to his ships. He made Tryon pay a heavy price for the damage done at Danbury.

On other occasions Tryon raided Fairfield, Norwalk and New Haven. In one skirmish, he battled against General Israel Putnam of Pomfret, a Connecticut hero who had fought at Bunker Hill. Among the men called to meet the attack on New Haven was President Doggett of Yale, who was wounded and taken prisoner by the British. Essex, New London and Stonington were raided by forces from British warships that were constantly cruising up and down the sound. Part of the garrison of Fort Griswold at Groton was massacred by the British after the fort had surrendered. On Tryon's last raid he met strong opposition and suffered heavy losses. This taught him a lesson and he stopped his raids.

Connecticut had much trouble with Tories in the first year or two of the war. Some of them served as spies for the British army. Laws were passed forbidding anyone to leave shore towns in a boat without permission. Strangers were not allowed to go from one town to another. Many Tories were sent to the copper mines at East Granby, which had been made a prison. In 1777 the General Assembly passed an act granting pardon to all Tories who were convinced of their errors. After the American victory at Saratoga, many Tories repented their errors and proclaimed their loyalty to the cause of liberty.

After the battle of Long Island, General Washington wanted to obtain information about enemy strength and positions. Such information could be obtained only by sending someone behind the enemy lines. Nathan Hale, a young graduate of Yale, volunteered for this dangerous service. Disguised as a schoolmaster, he went behind the British lines. Someone betrayed him; he was captured and hanged as a spy. Nathan Hale was one of

Winter on the Old North Road

Connecticut's heroes of the Revolution. His last words, "I only regret that I have but one life to give for my country," are the immortal words of a great patriot.

As the Revolution was drawing to a close, something happened which disturbed many people in Connecticut. In the middle of the morning of May 19, 1780, the sun was blotted out, and it began to grow dark. Chickens went to their roosts, and the wood thrush and whippoorwill began their evening calls.

No one knows what caused the Dark Day, as it was known for many years afterward. It might have been heavy smoke from distant forest fires. It might have been an eclipse of the sun, or a combination of the two. The darkness lasted until early afternoon, when it began to grow light again.

The most inspiring story of the Dark Day originated in Hartford, where the General Assembly was in session. As the light failed and the shadows deepened, some of the members became uneasy.

"I think the Day of Judgment is at hand," said one member in a shaky voice. "I move we adjourn."

Before the motion could be seconded, up rose the venerable Abraham Davenport of New Haven.

"Gentlemen," he said, "this is either the Day of Judgment or it is not. If it is not, there is no occasion for adjournment. If it is, I choose to be found doing my duty. I wish, therefore, that candles may be brought."

Chapter Eight

Growing Pains Of a New Country

The thirteen colonies did not become the United States of America right after the Revolutionary war ended with the surrender of General Cornwallis at Yorktown. For about four years Connecticut and the other states were unwilling to give up enough of their individual rights and powers to form a strong central government. It was a period of turmoil and confusion. Each state tried to issue its own money. Some states levied tariffs on almost everything, even firewood, that was sent in from other states. It was impossible to carry on much business under such conditions. Many people were unable to find work.

Gradually people began to realize that each state must be willing to give up some of its rights if it wanted to be part of a prosperous and peaceful nation. In 1787 delegates from all the states met in Philadelphia to draw up a constitution under which the group of separate states might join to become a strong country. Connecticut's delegates were Roger Sherman, Oliver Ellsworth and William Samuel Johnson. In January, 1788, the Connecticut General Assembly agreed to ratify the constitution. The group of states became the United States, and George Washington was elected to serve as the first president of the new nation.

Since its very earliest days Connecticut has had many men who wanted to get things done. They wanted to build ships and trade with other countries. They wanted to build roads, factories and canals. But while Connecticut was an English colony, there were many things they were not allowed to do. During the Revolution they were busy helping to win the war. In the first few years after the Revolution they were held back by a lack of sound money and by the trade restrictions imposed by the various states.

When trade barriers between the states were removed and a supply of sound money was assured, these Connecticut men could go ahead and do the things they had long wanted to do. Some of them wanted to build ships and trade with other countries. They knew Connecticut traders could sell lumber, livestock, grain and other products to people in the islands of the West Indies. They could buy sugar, molasses and rum, which would bring good prices in Connecticut.

Businessmen in Hartford, Farmington, New Haven, Norwich and other river or seaport towns built large sailing ships. Some of these were too big to sail all the way up the Connecticut River to Hartford. There were sandbars across the channel near Glastonbury, so Hartford ships were unloaded at Rocky Hill, which was then called Stepney. The Farmington River is much too shallow for large vessels, so Farmington ships were moored at Middletown. Their cargoes were loaded in wagons and hauled to town by way of Berlin, Kensington and Plainville, which was then known as White Oak.

Few businessmen could afford to build and equip a large sailing ship by themselves.

As a result, they sold shares of the ship to anyone who wanted to buy them. The value of a ship was divided into halves, quarters, eighths, sixteenths, thirty-seconds, sixty-fourths and one hundred twenty-eighths. If a ship cost $10,000 to build, a one hundred twenty-eighth share would cost about eighty dollars. Sometimes, on a single voyage, one of these ships would make a profit equal to its entire cost. People who had invested in a share of the cost would also share in the profits. It was rarely mentioned in public that many of these profitable voyages involved carrying slaves from Africa to the West Indies or the southern states. Some of the beautiful old houses in many Connecticut towns were paid for with profits earned from shares in seagoing ships.

Before the Revolution the few Connecticut people who traveled any great distance went by boat. Most of the roads between towns were little better than Indian trails. Madame Knight was one of the few women who ever made long journeys by land. In 1704 she traveled from Boston to New York by way of the Post Road, which was the best road in Connecticut at that time. But even the Post Road was too narrow and rough for wagons or carriages. She had to travel on horseback, and some of the bridges were so rickety that she was afraid both she and her horse might fall into the water.

Sleighs were used in Connecticut even in the early days of the colony, but until 1770, just a few years before the Revolution, wagons and carriages were seldom seen. Farmington did not see its first wagon until about 1772. A man named Cook bought one to carry his family to church. He did not have enough horses to carry them all on horseback, even when he put two children and one adult on each horse. His wagon created so much excitement when it first approached the church that Mr. Cook was arrested for disturbing the peace of the Sabbath. Probably that was Farmington's first traffic offense!

Litchfield saw its first carriage in 1776. A British officer, who was staying in a Litchfield home as a prisoner of war, brought his carriage with him when he came to town. Woodstock saw its first wagon in 1808 when Roger Huntington, of Windham, drove his wagon through town on his way to Leicester. It caused more excitement than a circus parade would today.

Serving in the army during the Revolution gave many men their first taste of travel. They learned that their own little town was not the only interesting place in the country. They found that people from other parts of the country were as friendly and courteous as their own neighbors, and they became more interested in travel.

Before people could do much traveling by land, there must be good roads. Building a road cost more than any one man could pay. Therefore, in order to build a turnpike, it was necessary to organize a company which could raise enough money to pay the costs of building the road. When the new road was opened, drivers of wagons, coaches and herds of cattle had to pay tolls. The toll collections were used to pay for the road and the company's profits. At each tollhouse a long stick, called a pike, blocked the road. After a driver had paid his toll, the pike was turned so that he could pass. Thus these roads came to be known as turnpikes.

While it was a colony, Connecticut itself was a company or corporation. At that time one company was not allowed to charter another. Only the king or a royal governor could

Transportation on the new Albany Turnpike, early 1800s

do that. Even though it was against the king's orders, Connecticut did charter one company while it was still a colony. That company was Yale College. Connecticut wanted a college to train its ministers, but it did not want to ask favors of the king. It quietly gave Yale a charter and hoped the king would not hear about it. Luckily, no one told him. If he had known, he might have been very angry.

When Connecticut became a state, the General Assembly was given the power to grant charters to groups of men who wanted to organize banks, build turnpikes or do other useful things. Between 1790 and 1800 many banking and turnpike companies were started. The banks made it easier for the turnpike companies to raise the large sums of money they needed.

The first turnpike to be built in Connecticut was the Norwich-New London road, known as the Mohegan Turnpike. Soon after this, the Hartford-New London road was built. It went through Glastonbury, Marlboro, Colchester and Salem. Next came the Hartford-New Haven turnpike, which went by way of Farmington, Southington, Cheshire and Hamden. Before this road was made a turnpike, it was known as the New Haven Path. Other important roads in early Connecticut were also called paths. They were well named. Men and animals could walk over them, but they were not fit for any kind of wagons or carriages.

One of the most interesting turnpikes was the Albany Turnpike. This was opened shortly before 1800. It followed much the same route as the Old North Road, and it soon became part of the easiest route from New England to the west. With the turnpikes came the stagecoaches. Nothing so large and comfortable had ever before been seen on Connecticut roads. The coaches that ran on western Connecticut roads, where the hills were long and steep, were often pulled by four horses which had to be kept running. The drivers liked to make the trip from Hartford to Albany, about a hundred miles, in one day. Sometimes the coach would leave Hartford at three o'clock in the morning and get into Albany after midnight. Before the turnpike was built the trip had taken two or three days. Long after stagecoaches had disappeared automobiles could travel the distance in two hours, and airplanes in about thirty-five minutes.

Horses could not be kept running hour after hour. Ten miles of steady running was enough to tire them. Soon taverns sprang up along the turnpikes, about ten miles apart. Here the coaches could stop and change horses. Passengers also welcomed these stops. Roads were dusty, and seats in the stagecoaches were not as comfortable as the seats in our cars. These stops gave the passengers a chance to stretch their legs and get a drink. If it happened to be mealtime, the coach would stop long enough for the passengers to have lunch or dinner.

The turnpikes brought travelers in and out of many towns where there had been no traffic before. People in these towns began to feel that now they were part of the world outside their own community. Before the days of the stagecoach it was impossible for anyone living in New Hartford or Hebron to go to Hartford and back the same day. If an individual had any business to do in Hartford, the round trip usually took about three days. With the coming of the stagecoach, he could make the trip in about two hours, take care of his business, and get home the same day. People living in Milford or Madison could now travel to New Haven and back, all in the same day.

Turnpike travelers had to stop at the tollgates, which were usually about ten miles apart. The toll charges on the Hartford-New London turnpike were four cents for a person and a horse or for an empty one-horse cart; six and one-fourth cents for a one-horse pleasure sleigh, an empty two-horse cart, or a loaded one-horse cart; twelve and a half cents for a chaise, sulky, or a loaded two-horse sleigh; twenty-five cents for a four wheeled pleasure carriage or a stagecoach; two cents for every horse, mule or cow; one-half cent for each sheep or pig.

Tolls were not collected from people going to church on Sunday or men on their way to do military training duty. Some people walked or drove around the outside edge of the tollhouse property to avoid paying the toll. The paths they made were called shunpikes.

Stagecoach travel cost about five or six cents a mile. This included the toll the driver had to pay. Along the Albany Turnpike, the stagecoach fare from Canton to Hartford was seventy-five cents. That may sound like a small amount of money, but at that time many farm workers earned only fifty cents a day, and a hired girl might be paid only a dollar for a whole week's work.

For many years Connecticut people were not allowed to travel on Sunday except to go to church. Stagecoach horses rested in their stables, trains stood still, and steamboats remained tied at their piers until after the sun went down.

However, as soon as the sun had set, the Sabbath was at an end, and people were free to do as they pleased. Sunday evening was a time when young men liked to call on their favorite young ladies. Such calls could never be made before sundown. An amusing story about courting tells of one Sunday evening when a young man wanted to visit the girl who later became his wife. She lived over the hill to the west of the valley where his farm was. He waited impatiently for the sun to disappear behind the hill. As soon as the last edge of the sun was out of sight, he rushed up the path that led to the young lady's home. Much to his surprise, when he reached the top of the hill he found the sun still shining on the other side. He had to sit down and wait, for he dared not go on until the sun had dropped beyond the distant hills.

Barges on the Farmington Canal

Chapter Nine

Barges, Railways and Steamboats

Why did Hartford and New Haven grow into towns and then become cities, while places such as Canterbury, Sharon and Voluntown remain small to this day? It was largely a matter of transportation. From the earliest days, boats could bring people and goods up the Connecticut River or into New Haven harbor. A town could grow to become a city only if good and inexpensive transportation made it easy to reach the town and to ship products and materials to and from the outside world.

During the half century or more that followed the Revolution, boats offered the cheapest and most convenient method of transportation. A boat could carry more passengers than a stagecoach and many more tons of freight than a wagon. In this period the towns that grew rapidly were those which were on navigable rivers or had good harbors.

Although Farmington was not on a navigable river, many of its people made money in shipping. They moored their ships in Middletown, more than fifteen miles away. Some people in Farmington thought that if passengers and freight could be brought into town by boat, Farmington would grow larger and richer than Hartford. They thought that if a canal could be dug from New Haven, on Long Island Sound, to Northampton, on the Connecticut River, it would bring many travelers and barge loads of merchandise to their town.

Hartford businessmen did not like the idea of a canal running from Northampton to New Haven. They were afraid the canal might draw traffic away from the Connecticut River. Some Hartford people were a bit jealous because Farmington people had made so much money in the shipping boom. People of New Haven, Cheshire and Farmington, who wanted the canal, wisely waited until the General Assembly met in New Haven before they asked for a charter. Hartford's representatives bitterly opposed it, but they were not strong enough to prevent the charter from being granted.

In a ceremony at Granby on July 4, 1825, Governor Wolcott was to break ground for the canal by turning the first shovelful of earth. The silver shovel broke, and that was only the first of a series of mishaps that befell the canal throughout its existence. The engineers who designed the canal allowed many small streams to flow into it, but they forgot to provide outlets where surplus water could drain out safely. When the small streams were flooded by heavy rains, the canal would begin to overflow its banks. Here and there a big gash would appear in the gravel bank, and all the water in that part of the canal would run out. Barges were left stuck in the mud, and farmers complained about all the water and gravel being washed across their fields.

In spite of these troubles many barges moved up and down the canal, towed by horses or mules that walked along the towpaths. The Albany Turnpike crossed the canal at Avon. Many wagon loads of freight came down the turnpike from northwestern Connecticut and were loaded on the barges in Avon. Axes from Collinsville, chairs from Riverton, sailcloth from New Hartford, and iron, limestone and lumber from as far away as Salisbury were put aboard the barges there. Avon became a busy port. The freight was shipped to New Haven where some of it was put on large sailing ships and sent to the West Indies, Nova Scotia, Baltimore or Savannah.

Barges coming up from New Haven might be loaded with coal for the Collins Company, bricks that had been made in New Haven, or rum, molasses and sugar which seagoing ships had brought to New Haven. Farmington is about halfway between Northampton and New Haven. Expecting that many travelers using the canal would want to spend the night there, Farmington built a big brick hotel on Main Street. But soon the barges had comfortable sleeping quarters. Travelers found it more convenient and less expensive to spend the night on the barge. The hotel became the main building of Miss Porter's School.

People who bought or sold loads of heavy freight liked the canal because it saved them money. The Collins Company, which made axes, had a lot of coal shipped by barge from New Haven to Avon. The cost was about twenty-five cents a ton for shipping it forty miles on a canal barge. Then it was hauled by wagons to Collinsville, about five miles from Avon. It cost seventy-five cents a ton to haul that coal five miles in wagons.

Growing boys liked the canal, too. There were a great many fish in it. It was deep enough for swimming but not deep enough to be dangerous. A favorite sport for boys in the towns along the canal was to drop to the deck of a passing barge from one of the low bridges that crossed the canal, ride a few miles, then pull themselves up on another bridge and wait for a barge to carry them back home.

Among the many things that troubled the canal was cold weather. Often it would be covered with ice for four months of the year. It was a wonderful place to skate. Sometimes in the evening people would skate from Farmington to Simsbury, have dinner there, and skate home again. But the canal company could not collect a toll from skaters. Factory owners, storekeepers and travelers could not use the canal when it was covered with ice. They wanted transportation that was faster and more dependable than a canal barge. The railroad provided just that. In 1839 Connecticut completed its first railroad, which ran between Hartford and New Haven. It was so successful that in 1848 the water was drained from the canal, and a railroad was built over its right of way. It was called the Canal Line.

John Fitch, the first man in America to make a boat run by steam, was born in South Windsor, Connecticut. In 1785 he built a model of a boat that was pushed through the water by paddle wheels. Two years later he tried out a steam-powered boat that reached a speed of about four miles an hour. In 1790 he was operating a steamboat on the Delaware River, carrying passengers between Philadelphia and Trenton. This boat could travel more than seven miles an hour. But luck ran against John Fitch. He had difficulty raising the money he needed, and other men were given credit for some of his discoveries. About twenty years after Fitch made his first successful run, Robert Fulton launched a steamboat that ran between Albany and New York City.

Long before 1824 there could have been regular steamboat service between New York and such Connecticut ports as Stonington, Norwich, Hartford, New Haven and Bridgeport, except for one thing. New York passed a law that no one but Fulton could operate steamboats in New York waters. Connecticut people were so angry about this that they passed a law forbidding the use of Connecticut waters by steamboats which belonged to anyone in New York. For many years no steamboats could run from Connecticut ports to New York City. Finally, in 1824, the Supreme Court decided that no state could prevent the use of its waters by steamboats from other states if Congress had passed laws permitting such use. Then many steamboats began to run between New York and Connecticut ports.

Through the years, children thoroughly enjoyed the Connecticut River steamboats. Sometimes several boys would go aboard the "Hartford" or the "Middletown" when the boat docked at Hartford. They would pay five cents to ride as far as Glastonbury, where each boat made its first stop. Then they would get on a trolley car and, for another five-cent fare, ride back to Hartford. It cost only a dime for a whole afternoon of fun. Older boys, paddling canoes on the river, looked forward to meeting a steamboat. The waves it created could make a canoe ride wet but exciting.

Even business travelers found that the river steamers offered a delightful, unhurried trip to and from New York. The ship sailed from Hartford at five o'clock in the afternoon. Usually, by the time she reached Middletown, dinner was ready. The food was well prepared and nicely served by waiters wearing freshly laundered white jackets. On long summer evenings the scenery along the river was beautiful. The boat stopped at several landings, and the stevedores sometimes sang as they loaded boxes and bales aboard the steamer. Soon after passing the Cornfield Point lightship out in the sound, most passengers went to bed. The cabins were large and clean, and the beds were comfortable. The constant sea breezes kept passengers cool, even when the weather on shore was very hot.

The boat docked in New York at about six o'clock in the morning. Passengers could have breakfast on board, go ashore to keep their business appointments, and return at the end of the day to spend another night on the boat. The next morning would find them back in Hartford, well rested and ready for a new day's work.

Connecticut's first railroad ran only between Hartford and New Haven. It was not possible at that time to go all the way to New York by train. The building of the shoreline railroad was delayed for several years because of wide estuaries along the shore, which required large ferries or long bridges.

In cold weather, when the Connecticut River froze, the river boats could not run. Between 1824 and 1839 anyone who wanted to go from Hartford to New York in winter took a sleigh or stagecoach from Hartford to New Haven and boarded a steamer there. Only once has there been a winter so cold that the salt water of Long Island froze from shore to shore. After railroad service began between Hartford and New Haven, travelers could take a train that left Hartford in the evening and made connections with the boat at New Haven. The boat sailed at ten o'clock and arrived in New York the next morning. The train was very convenient for people in the Hartford area, especially during winter months when ice blocked the Connecticut River.

The Hartford-New Haven railroad proved that trains were more comfortable and less expensive than stagecoaches, and faster than canal barges or steamboats. Trains could run day or night during any season of the year, and soon every town in Connecticut wanted a railroad running close to it. (Some people objected to having a railroad too close. Miss Sarah Porter did not want trains running through her school property in Farmington. She insisted that the railroad tracks be laid on the west side of the river, two miles from town. For many years a stagecoach carried passengers from the station to the village.)

By 1870, Connecticut was so crisscrossed by railroad lines that nearly every town in the state had a railroad station. Some had two. Hartford was like a great octopus, with six different lines running in and out of the city.

Chapter Ten

The Westward Trek

In the early days Connecticut farms had to be large. They had to provide food for the whole family, pasture lands and winter supplies for the livestock, enough flax to make plenty of linen for sheets and shirts, and a large supply of wood to keep the family warm through the winter months and to cook their meals throughout the entire year. Only those towns with wide expanses of rich bottom lands could have more than three or four farms on each square mile of town land.

Towns were usually no more than six miles from one end to the other. If a town were any larger than that, farmers living on the outskirts could not haul a load of grain to the mill near the center of town, have it ground into meal or flour, and get back home in time to do the chores.

This meant that few Connecticut towns had more than a hundred farms large enough to support a family in comfort. Families were large. Often there were eight or ten children, or even more. The oldest son was usually expected to stay on the farm when his father grew too old to do the work. The other boys in the family would have to find farms somewhere else or find some other way of earning a living. In any town that had been settled for more than a few years it was hard to find good farm land for sale at a reasonable price. The original settlers had usually divided all the good land among themselves when they first arrived.

There were some ways, other than farming, by which a man could earn a living. Each town needed a minister, a doctor, a storekeeper, one or two blacksmiths, and perhaps two or three millers. But these jobs could be filled by a very small number of people. Often the minister and the doctor had to do some farming also, because they could not earn enough to take care of their families by preaching or practicing medicine.

If the younger boys in a family wanted a farm, the wisest thing they could do was to join some company that was heading west where, until about 1900, they were sure to find some vacant land.

The westward migration began in earliest colonial days. Even the settlement of Windsor, Hartford and Wethersfield was part of the movement. These towns were founded by people who felt crowded in the Plymouth and Massachusetts Bay colonies. All the good farm land there had been taken by the first settlers. Those who came later had to move west to the Connecticut River valley to find good land they could afford to buy.

Some other long westward treks were made early in the history of the colonies. In 1639 Roger Ludlow and eight or nine families from Windsor began the settlement of Stratford and Fairfield. Two years later settlers from Wethersfield, under the leadership of the Reverend Richard Denton, started the town of Stamford. Some members of the

New Haven colony were just as eager to move into the wide open spaces and in 1639 Guilford and Milford were settled by people from New Haven.

Frequently people from two or more settlements would join in establishing a new town. Harwinton was settled by people from Hartford, Windsor and Farmington. They coined the name of their town from a syllable in the name of each of the parent towns. People from Windsor, Farmington and Simsbury used the same idea when they settled Wintonbury, now called Bloomfield. In later years people from Barkhamsted started a manufacturing town on the banks of Mad River in the town of Winchester. They named it Winsted.

Beginning with Windsor as an example, the pattern of westward migration can be easily traced. Within twenty years after Windsor was settled, many of the children had grown up, and the town became crowded. A group of Windsor people made their way over Talcott Mountain and founded Simsbury. After another twenty years all the good farm land in Simsbury had been taken. A new crop of boys was coming of age, so they moved five or six miles to the west and founded Canton. By the end of the next twenty year period, Canton had a number of boys looking for farms or other ways to earn a living. About fifteen miles west of Canton they founded Torrington and Colebrook. By the time Colebrook's boys reached the age when they were ready to look for farms, much of Connecticut had been settled, and it was necessary to go hundreds of miles into western New York, Pennsylvania or Vermont to find vacant lands.

The girls in small towns did not like the idea of so many of the boys going west. It often meant that the number of girls looking for husbands was much greater than the number of boys left in the town. It was not considered proper for a girl to leave home and look for a job in some distant town. Also, there were not the many different kinds of jobs that women fill today. Until the time of the Civil War, almost the only job a woman could get, away from her own home, was the job of hired girl in some other woman's home. That was not very interesting. Sometimes a girl would solve this problem by marrying the boy she loved and braving the hardships of the long trip west with him. Another might wait until her boy found a farm and came back to get her, but sometimes the boy found another girl along the way and never came back. Some of the girls who remained unmarried spent their whole lives in the homes where they were born, spinning, weaving churning butter and doing other household tasks.

Several companies of Hessian soldiers, captured at Saratoga, were marched through western Connecticut as prisoners of war. Often, when a company reached Hartford, there were fewer in the group than when it left Greenbush, near Albany. Some were helped to escape by girls who were looking for husbands. In Canton there is a house which was built by an escaped Hessian prisoner. He married the girl who helped him escape, and it is said that they lived happily ever after.

Soon after 1800 someone devised a new type of water wheel which made it possible to harness such rivers as the Connecticut, the Farmington and the Housatonic. The good power sites on these rivers were often the rugged, rocky stretches which had been thinly settled because they included few acres suitable for farming.

Around 1820 several small manufacturing towns began to spring up along the larger rivers. At that time the French word "ville", meaning town, was quite popular. Many of the new mill towns were given names that ended with ville. Collinsville, Unionville and Tariffville came into being along the Farmington River between 1825 and 1840. Hitchcockville, named after the famous chair manufacturer, got off to a bad start as far as its name was concerned. Mail addressed to the chair factory often went to Hotchkissville, so the name of the town was changed to Riverton.

Connecticut people liked to settle on lands to which they thought their state had a lawful claim. Connecticut's charter had given the colony a claim to a strip of land fifty or sixty miles wide, which stretched from the Atlantic Ocean to the Pacific. Such property was very valuable, and perhaps that was one of the reasons why Connecticut had refused to part with its charter.

The strip of land crossed New York, but the grant given to the Duke of York so clearly included this section of the strip that Connecticut made no effort to claim it. There was a question about Connecticut's right to the section that ran across northern Pennsylvania. The charter given to William Penn appeared to include that land.

The Pennsylvanians were thought to be a peaceful people. In 1754 five or six hundred people from Windham County formed the Susquehanna Company and traveled west to settle on the Pennsylvania section of Connecticut's strip of land. Agents of the company bought a large piece of property on the Susquehanna and Delaware rivers. The land was bought from the Indian tribes known as the Five Nations. Within the next few years settlements were made first along the Delaware, then on the Susquehanna. The Susquehanna settlement was called Westmoreland, a name that was considered likely to attract new settlers. In 1776 Westmoreland was made a Connecticut county. Connecticut laws were enforced there, and Connecticut taxes had to be paid.

Many Pennsylvania people were not willing to let Connecticut claim this large part of what they considered their land. Westmoreland men who were serving in the army were afraid there might be trouble. They asked permission to return to their homes, but the Continental Congress refused to let them go. In July, 1778, a large band of Tories and Indians attacked Westmoreland. The only defenders were men too old to serve in the army and boys who were too young. They fought bravely until most of them were killed or wounded. The women and children had to make the long journey back to Connecticut, and the Westmoreland County of Connecticut went out of existence.

Although the westward migration to Pennsylvania was unsuccessful, no other state had a claim on the section of the Connecticut strip which passed through northern Ohio. This became known as the Western Reserve. After the Revolution many people from Connecticut settled there.

After the Erie Canal was completed, wheat, corn and cattle from the fertile fields of New York, Ohio and other western states began to pour into eastern cities. Because the western fields were flat and free from rocks, it cost much less to raise food there than on the thin, stone-filled soil of Connecticut's hill farms. Food prices in eastern markets began to fall. Soon people could buy western products for less than it cost to raise the same things in Connecticut. Many Connecticut farmers abandoned their hill farms and went west to find more fertile land. When Connecticut farmers heard news of the discovery of gold in California, hundreds of them went to seek their fortunes in the far west. Few found much gold, but many of them found farm lands that were better than those they had left.

For people of southern New England the Albany Turnpike was a favorite route to the west. Except for some steep hills in western Connecticut, this route made it possible to get to the midwest without climbing over high mountains. Travelers followed the turnpike to Albany and then went along the Mohawk Valley to the shores of the Great Lakes. Many families built large wagons with canvas tops which kept out the rain. These covered wagons, or prairie schooners, served as tents for the family to sleep in at night. Some days the people of Norfolk, Canaan and other towns along the Albany Turnpike would see dozens of covered wagons rolling toward the west.

Chapter Eleven

Early Connecticut Industries

For almost two hundred years farming was the chief occupation of most men in towns such as Pomfret, Cornwall and Southbury, which are not close to deep rivers or the coast. In Westbrook, Lyme, Waterford and other small shore towns some men earned part of their living by fishing, digging clams, and catching crabs and lobsters. Hartford, Middletown, Norwich and New Haven had some men who were sailors, shipbuilders or sailmakers. But most of the people in early Connecticut were farmers.

Farming during that period was quite different from farming today. A modern Connecticut farmer usually raises one crop, or markets one product, and buys all the other things his family needs. The early farmers had to know how to do many things. They had to build their own houses and barns. They had to cut trees for lumber and firewood. They had to build stone walls and fences. They made many of their own tools, including wagons, sleighs and stone boats. Some of them made the furniture they used in their homes. They plowed the land, sowed the seeds, and harvested the crops.

Their wives and daughters had to know how to do as many things as the men did. They spun the flax and wool, then wove it into cloth. They cut and sewed most of the clothes the family wore. They churned butter and made cheese. They dipped candles, salted down the pork, and cured the bacon. In the early spring they boiled the maple sap to make syrup or maple sugar. Every day, of course, they also cooked the meals, made the beds, swept the floors and took care of the children. Before 1800 there were few factories in Connecticut. The home was the factory which produced most of the things the people needed.

The early settlers had no gasoline engines or electric motors to help them do their work. But they knew how to dam their small streams and make them turn water wheels. The water wheels could be hooked up to a saw or a pair of grindstones. This made it easier to cut beams and boards or grind corn and wheat. Their saws moved up and down in much the same way a saw does when it is being used by hand. Later they learned to make a water wheel turn a circular saw. Experts can tell the age of an old board by looking at the marks of the saw. If the marks are straight across the board, it was probably cut by one of the early up-and-down saws. The board is not so old if it shows the curved marks made by a circular saw.

Most of the mills that were built near the falls or rapids in the larger streams were grist mills or sawmills. In addition to these there were fulling mills which cleaned the grease from homespun woolen cloth and treated it so it would not shrink, dish mills which made wooden plates, and mills which made lye from wood ashes. The women used lye to make waste fat into soap. In a few small mills the water wheel was made to turn a lathe and work a small saw. In this kind of mill a master craftsman and his apprentice would make harvest tables, Windsor chairs, spool beds and other furniture. In some of the larger towns there were shops where an apprentice had to supply the power for the machines by turning a large wheel by hand or by pedaling with his feet. Until after the Revolution most of the mills and shops were small, rarely employing more than three or four men. Often one or two of these men were apprentices who had promised to work for seven years with no pay except their board and room and, perhaps, a suit of clothes or a few dollars at the end of the seven years. They did this in order to learn the trade. After serving seven years as an apprentice, a man was considered a skilled worker, and he could earn better pay, perhaps as much as a dollar a day.

There was a good reason why there were no large factories in those days. A great deal of power is needed to operate a factory in which hundreds of people work on many machines. The overshot water wheels used by the early mills and shops were easy to build and very dependable. But one of these wheels could operate only one set of grinding stones or one saw, and only one or two men were needed to keep those stones or that saw busy. These small mills could not provide jobs for a large number of workers. The brooks and streams did not provide enough power at any one place to operate many machines.

But there was a lot of water power going to waste in Connecticut. In the falls and rapids of the larger rivers there was enough power to turn a great many machines. Some of the early settlers knew this. They hated to have this power go to waste when there was so much work to be done. But they did not dam the big rivers because there was no water wheel that could make use of the large amount of water. Then, around 1800, someone invented such a wheel.

France and England were at war at this time. Their warships were capturing American merchant ships. A law was passed forbidding American ships to leave port. Trading with other countries became unprofitable and often impossible. Connecticut businessmen began to look for other ways to make money. They heard about the new water wheel. They knew there were many rapids on the larger rivers. They soon learned that the new water wheel could run machines which would shred rags to make paper, or spin thread and weave it into rolls of cloth. Many lathes and small saws could be turned by one of these big new wheels, and Lambert Hitchcock could offer jobs to dozens of men in his furniture factory at Riverton. As soon as men found this new source of power, machines were quickly designed to stamp out clock wheels, brass buttons, axe heads and many other things. Between 1820 and 1840 many new factories were started in Connecticut.

It took time for large groups of men to learn to work together to make clocks, axes, chairs, sailcloth or carpets. Never before had men done this. They had fought together in armies and worked together on ships, but never before had a man spent all his time running a machine that did just one little part of making a clock or a chair. When spring came, many of the workers in the axe factory at Collinsville wanted to leave their jobs so they could plant their gardens. Samuel Collins had to work hard to convince them that it would be better for them to stay on their jobs and buy the vegetables they needed.

Cotton was a very expensive fiber until Eli Whitney, a Connecticut man, invented the cotton gin in 1792. It cost a lot of money to have the seeds combed out of the cotton bolls by hand. When the cotton gin made it easy to remove the seeds, the price of cotton cloth was lower, and there was a great demand for it. Many mills were built to meet this demand. There were cotton mills at Colebrook River, New Hartford and Avon.

Most of the water-powered factories in northwestern Connecticut were owned by Connecticut people. But the Greenwoods cotton mill in New Hartford was built by a group of New York shipowners who needed thousands of yards of strong canvas for the sails of their ships. Canvas sails made in New Hartford were the wings that captured the wind to carry fast American clipper ships all over the world. When steam engines took the place of sails, the Greenwoods mill began to lay off its workers. One of its last large orders was for canvas for the tents of Buffalo Bill's Wild West Show. The mill closed around 1900, and it took New Hartford many years to recover from the loss of its largest industry.

There were paper mills at Riverton, Unionville and Poquonock on the Farmington River, at Windsor Locks on the Connecticut, and at Rockville on the Hockanum River. Paper was made from linen and cotton rags. Sometimes an enterprising immigrant bought a horse and wagon soon after arriving in this country. He drove through the streets and back roads, buying rags. His simple chant was heard again and again, "Cash paid for rags." The rags he collected cost him a few pennies here and there, but at the paper mill he found a ready market for them. Some of the men who started out as rag collectors became very wealthy and left large fortunes to their children.

In 1828 a water-powered mill, designed for weaving carpets, was started in the eastern part of Simsbury. Soon a village grew up around it. The mill produced fine carpets, but European factories sold their carpets in the United States for less than the prices of rugs made at the Connecticut mill. Time after time the owners of the mill begged Congress to levy a tariff on imported carpets. The mill village had no name, but when it grew so large that it had to have a post office, a name had to be chosen. While different names were being considered, the people were notified that Congress had granted their request for the tariff. They were so pleased that they called their village Tariffville.

In 1789 Eli Terry, of Watertown, began to make clocks. Wood was the only material he had for making clock wheels. Cutting the wheels from wood was a delicate and tiresome process. For that reason wooden wheeled clocks were very expensive.

Sometimes when one of these clocks was shipped by boat or used in a shore town, the damp air would cause the wooden wheels to warp. Then the clock would not keep good time. It would run too fast or too slow, or perhaps it would refuse to run at all. Then another clockmaker, Chauncey Jerome, tried making clock wheels from an old brass kettle. The clock ran very well, not only in central Connecticut where the air was usually dry, but also near the shore where fog often made the air damp. Brass does not warp or rust.

Compared with iron or steel, brass is a soft metal. The new water wheel could turn big rollers which would roll the brass into sheets just the right thickness for clock wheels. Then another machine could stamp the wheels out of the brass sheets. Each wheel would be exactly the right size, and the machine could turn out hundreds of wheels in the time it took to make one wheel from wood. This made it possible to produce a clock that could be sold for about five dollars, which was much less than the cost of a clock with wooden wheels.

In those days there were no factory whistles or radio time signals, and soon almost every family in Connecticut wanted to buy one of these new clocks. For a while the clock factories in Winsted, Thomaston and Terryville had plenty of orders to keep them busy. One of the clock companies which developed after 1840 was started by Elias Ingraham, a cabinetmaker. The E. Ingraham Company still exists today and is known for its timepieces.

But the time came when clocks had been sold to nearly everyone in the state who could afford to buy one. Then the clockmakers had to send salesmen all over the country to look for buyers. These salesmen were the famous Yankee peddlers. They drove wagons with teams of two horses each. The wagons were boxed in to protect the clocks from weather and thieves. Wherever there were settlers, the peddlers would go. Even before 1840 they were going as far west as Arkansas and Missouri. If a frontier family had no money to pay for a clock, the peddler would sometimes take furs, homespun cloth or tanned hides in trade. Often these settlers who lived in the wilderness were glad to give a Connecticut clock peddler a night's lodging and one or two meals, just to hear the news he could tell of the outside world.

In 1842, Chauncey Jerome went a step further and shipped some metal clocks overseas. He contracted with a Mr. Epaphroditus Peck of Bristol to take a shipload of one-day brass clocks to England. Neighboring clockmakers laughed at Jerome for doing this. They told him he was foolish to send clocks because the English were against buying American products. Also, labor was cheaper in England, probably making the price of their own clocks lower than his. Nevertheless, he sent Mr. Peck and Chauncey Jerome Jr. across the Atlantic with the clocks. The first year no clocks were sold. As had been predicted, Yankee goods were not wanted in England. Chauncey Jerome would not give up. Finally a merchant grudgingly took two clocks to sell. The next day when Epaphroditus Peck and young Jerome returned to the store, the clocks had been sold. The merchant took four more, which were sold by the next day. Then he ordered a dozen more. It seemed that although American clocks were cheaper, they were well made and could sell.

Further, according to Chauncey Jerome, the customs officials learned that the clocks, though inexpensive, were good. A regulation of the Customs House allowed the seller to set his price on incoming goods. The customs officers seized one shipload of clocks because of the low price and then paid for them. That didn't bother Chauncey Jerome too much, because he received payment. The customs officials seized a second load and paid again, adding ten per cent to the cost. Mr. Jerome thought this was an easy way to sell his clocks. He sent another shipload, but this time the clocks were let through as the Customs House officials finally realized that the Americans could produce better clocks for a lower price.

Among the early enterprises in Connecticut were the newspapers. The Connecticut

Gazette, founded in New Haven in 1755 by James Parker, was the first newspaper in the colony. Before 1800 thirty-five other papers were started. From those early days to the present time people's lives and opinions have been influenced by the news, editorials and advertising which have appeared in newspapers.

The Connecticut Courant was founded in 1764 by Thomas Green. Now known as The Hartford Courant, it has become famous as America's oldest newspaper in continuous circulation. In 1796 the Courant carried two advertisements which were paid for by George Washington. The Courant is the oldest business firm operating in Connecticut. Only fourteen active businesses in the United States are older; almost five million are newer.

Ship loading cargo bound for the West Indies

Chapter Twelve

How Hartford Became The Insurance City

It is hard to believe it now, but Hartford was once a busy shipping port. Many ships were owned by Hartford people. These ships depended on sails and wind power, for steam engines had not yet come into common use.

Now and then a sailing vessel would get into trouble. She might be driven ashore in a storm, run into another ship in a fog, or lose her masts in a gale. Often, a ship might be owned by just one or two men who had paid a great deal of money for her. If their ship were lost, the owners might have no money with which to buy a new one, and they might be forced out of the shipping business. Ship owners wished for some way of protecting their investments against such losses.

Some men in London had found a way to offer such protection. They devised a plan whereby individuals would be paid ten dollars when they in turn agreed to pay a hundred dollars if a named ship were lost on her next voyage. The chance that a ship might be lost on an ordinary voyage was much less than one in ten. If a person took chances on a ship, he was almost certain to make money. Should a ship be planning to make a dangerous trip, more than ten dollars would have to be paid to individuals agreeing to pay one hundred dollars if she were lost. Thus began the famous "Lloyd's of London."

A man named Ezekial Williams heard about this system and decided to try the same idea in Hartford. If a shipowner wanted to insure his ship before it set sail on a voyage, Ezekial would write on a paper the names of the ship and her captain, the value of the ship, and her destination. Ezekial would pass the paper among wealthy men in Hartford. Any man who wished to invest in part of the insurance for this ship would write, under the description of the ship, his name and the amount of money he was willing to risk. If he wanted to risk one hundred dollars, he would be paid ten dollars. If he were willing to risk one thousand dollars, he would be paid a hundred dollars. If the ship returned safely from its voyage, the man would keep the money he had received. Of course, if the ship were lost, he would have to pay her owners the amount of money he had agreed to risk. Most of the ships returned safely, and the men who insured them collected more money than they had to pay out for lost ships. They were called underwriters because they signed their names under the description of each ship they insured. Some insurance men are still called underwriters.

Ezekial Williams was Hartford's first insurance man. However, his system involved several problems. He often had to spend weeks talking to a great many men before he was able to insure the full value of a ship. His underwriters knew the names of the ships they were insuring, and on stormy nights they often lay awake, worrying about the danger of shipwrecks. If a ship failed to return safely from its voyage, Ezekial sometimes had difficulty collecting the money the underwriters had agreed to risk. The underwriters would finally pay their losses because if they didn't, people would not continue to do business with them. But often it took Ezekial a long time to settle an insurance claim for a lost vessel.

The Hartford Marine Insurance Company was formed, and Ezekial no longer had to search for men who would risk money to insure ships. The company raised money by selling shares in its business. When it had plenty of money with which to work, it began selling insurance. When a shipowner asked an agent of the company to insure his ship for $10,000, the agent would say, "If our experts think your ship is a good risk, you may buy the insurance. We will let you know tomorrow." Shipowners liked this quick service. Men who owned shares in the company seldom knew the names and destinations of the ships their company had insured; they did not worry so much about the danger of shipwrecks in stormy weather. When a ship was lost, it was easier for the owner to settle his claim with one company than with twenty or thirty individual underwriters.

The Hartford Marine Insurance Company, which was Hartford's first insurance company, was successful for six or eight years. Then France and England started fighting again, and both began to capture American ships. To prevent the United States from being drawn into the war, President Thomas Jefferson ordered that American ships must not leave port. When Hartford's ships were forbidden to leave the Connecticut River, the shipowners needed no insurance, and the Hartford Marine Company went out of business.

While Hartford was a small town, people felt no need to insure their homes against fire. Everyone knew everyone else. If a man's house or barn burned, his friends and neighbors would help him rebuild it. They would look in their attics for furniture he could use. People did this because they knew that they, too, would need help if fire destroyed their property. It was a kind of unwritten fire insurance.

When Connecticut towns began to grow larger, it was impossible for everyone in town to know everyone else. Some people built big houses and bought expensive rugs and furniture. If such a house burned down, it could not easily be rebuilt by neighbors, and old chests and tables from a friend's attic were not satisfactory substitutes for fine imported furnishings.

People began to look for some way to insure their homes against fire. In our country, where everyone is free to start any lawful business, someone is certain to recognize a growing need for a new product or service. So it happened in Hartford. In 1810 the first fire insurance company was organized.

The men who first offered to sell fire insurance had a great deal to learn. They did not realize that a whole city might burn in one fire, causing their company heavy losses. They did not realize that part of every dollar they were paid should be set aside to provide for such disasters. At the end of each year, after all claims and expenses had been paid, they divided the remaining money among the stockholders who owned shares in the company. If the stockholders received big dividends, they might celebrate with a party. But as the new year began, the company would have no money on hand. If someone reported a fire loss in January, he could not collect his insurance until the company took in enough money to pay the claim. If a big fire destroyed many buildings insured by the company, claims would be paid until all the company's cash had been used. Then an agent would say, "We are very sorry, but we have no more money. We cannot pay any more claims. We are out of business." Many people who had bought insurance found that their policies were worthless.

In 1835 Eliphalet Terry was made president of the first Hartford company to write fire insurance. He was not satisfied with the way the fire insurance business was being run. He felt that it was wrong for a company to go out of business because it did not have enough money to pay its claims. He believed a company should do everything possible to make sure it would have money for all claims.

As the end of 1835 drew near, Terry's company had a large amount of money on hand. It appeared that the stockholders would receive a big dividend for that year. Then news came that much of New York City had been destroyed in a great fire. The company's losses amounted to $60,000, which was far more than the profits the company had earned during the year. A meeting of the directors was called.

"What shall we do?" one man asked anxiously.

"Do?" answered Terry. "There is only one thing for us to do. We will pay the claims, even if it takes every dollar I have in this world. I have already pledged my property for a loan at the bank. I am leaving for New York by sleigh right after this meeting. I will pay every loss as long as I have a dollar left."

When Terry reached New York, everything was in confusion. All the other companies which had insured buildings in the burned area had gone out of business because they were unable to pay their claims.

Terry climbed on a pile of bricks, and a crowd quickly gathered around him. "My company will pay every dollar of its losses," said Terry. "And we will be happy to accept new insurance. We are still in business, and we intend to stay in business."

Then an amazing thing happened. Some people claimed the money their policies provided, but many more came forward to buy insurance from this company which was proving that it would pay, even when its losses were great. Money came in faster than it went out. When Terry had paid all the claims, he went back to Hartford with a lot of money in his sleigh.

People quickly spread the news that Terry's company was able to pay all its losses in a fire which caused the failure of many other companies. Hundreds of people wanted to buy insurance from such a company, and many men wanted to become its agents. But most important of all, other Connecticut insurance companies learned that they must follow the example set by Eliphalet Terry. They must run their businesses so that they would have money to pay all claims, even when there were heavy losses.

Today there are many different kinds of insurance companies in Connecticut. About forty insurance companies have their offices in Hartford. They have grown successfully because people know they can be depended upon to carry out their promises.

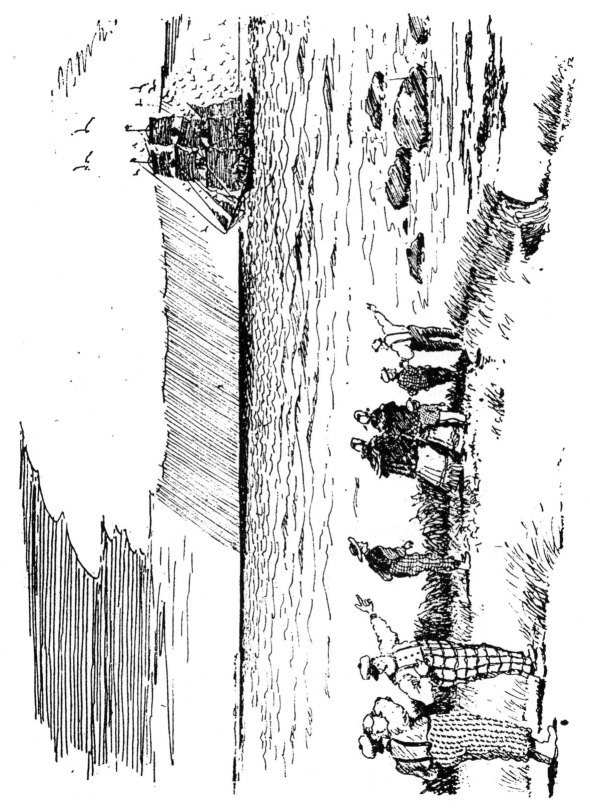

The Amistad, suspicious looking vessel that appeared off the shores of Long Island

54

Chapter Thirteen

The Capture of The Amistad

If you should visit the cemetery on Garden Street in Farmington, you would find a time-worn gravestone which bears the following inscription:

Foone

A native African who was drowned while bathing in the Centre Basin, Aug. 1841. He was one of the Company of Slaves under Cinque on board the Schooner Amistad who asserted their rights and took possession of the vessel after having put the Captain, Mate and others to death, sparing their masters Ruiz and Montez.

This is a reminder of the part Connecticut played in a story as colorful and exciting as any tale of pirates on the high seas. Also, it was one of the events that led to the Civil War and the end of slavery about twenty-five years later.

In August 1839, fishermen and country folk who lived along the beaches at the eastern end of Long Island were puzzled and disturbed by the appearance of a suspicious looking vessel. She was a schooner, evidently of foreign registry, with rakish masts and tattered rigging. Painted black, she lay low in the water.

Men who had been able to get near her said that both her captain and her crew were Negroes, but it was hard to learn anything more about her. She would veer away whenever a boat came near her. Residents of the little fishing villages near Montauk warned their children not to stray far from home. At night they locked their doors. They sent a message asking the Coast Guard to investigate.

A few days later the brig Washington, of the United States Coast Guard, sighted the mysterious craft lying at anchor off Culloden Point. She appeared to be taking on supplies and water. An armed boat was sent to take possession of her. She offered no resistance to the boarding party, but her captain, an African prince by the name of Cinque, jumped overboard and started swimming out to sea. The boat crew had to lasso him before they were able to bring him aboard. Later he told them that he did not want to be taken alive because he felt certain that he would be hanged.

The strange vessel proved to be the Amistad, of Havana. At the time of her capture she was commanded and manned by Negroes. Imprisoned below deck were two white men, Don Jose Ruiz and Don Pedro Montez. They greeted the American sailors with great joy. From their stories and the story told by Cinque, the tale of the black Mendis and the Amistad began to unfold.

The Mendis were a tribe who lived on the west coast of Africa. Although they were far too independent and warlike to make good slaves, some of them were captured by slave hunters, sold to Portuguese slave traders, and transported in the slave ship, Tecova, to Havana. There they were sold to Don Ruiz and Don Montez.

These two men chartered the Amistad to take the Mendis to a port near their plantations in Cuba. Because the Mendis seemed quite friendly, they were not confined but were given the run of the ship. Four days out of Havana one of them asked the cook where they were going and what was going to happen to them. The cook made motions indicating that he was going to kill and eat them. They did not realize that he was joking, and the idea did not seem very funny to them. The Mendis got together and decided that if any killing were to be done, they would rather be the killers than the victims. That night they swarmed up on deck and killed the captain after he had first killed one of them. Then they threw the cook overboard and seized the ship.

Cinque, the leader of the mutiny, ordered that Ruiz and Montez be spared. He intended to sail directly back to Africa, and he knew he would need the help of the white men. On his westbound voyage from Africa to Havana aboard the Tecova, Cinque had noticed that each day the sun rose astern of the ship and set ahead of it. "If we sail so the sun rises ahead of us and sets behind us," he said to himself, "we will find our way home." However, he knew nothing about steering by the stars or using the mariner's compass, so he planned to depend on the two white men to keep the ship on her course at night. If Ruiz and Montez had happened to want to go to Africa, Cinque's plan might have worked very well. But Africa was the last place either of them wanted to see.

During the daylight hours Cinque would steer the ship toward the east. But as soon as it grew dark and the wheel was turned over to him, Montez, who had spent part of his life at sea, would ease the ship around and head her into the west. Several times Cinque became suspicious and threatened to kill the two white men. The night before the Amistad was captured they were afraid Cinque was about to carry out his threat. After sighting the Montauk light, Montez had tried to run the ship aground on the point, but he was a few minutes too late. The flood tide was running fast, and the ship was carried into the bay.

The captured Amistad was escorted into New London by the Washington. She had hardly dropped anchor when the Spanish minister claimed that Cinque and all his African companions were the lawful property of Don Ruiz and Don Montez. He demanded that they be turned over to their white masters for punishment. Southern slaveholders and some people in the north agreed with the Spanish minister.

This outraged many people not only in Connecticut but also throughout New England. They pointed out that slave trade was forbidden under the laws of both the United States and Spain. They said the African captives had been unlawfully held aboard the Amistad, and it was within their rights to strike for freedom. Many Connecticut people admired the brave effort Cinque had made to keep his people from becoming slaves, and they became strong defenders of the Mendis.

"The most famous case ever tried in Connecticut was that of the Amistad," wrote Simeon E. Baldwin in 1888. "None ever awakened a wider interest or deeper feeling. I think we may fairly deem it one of the first guideposts that pointed the way to the yet

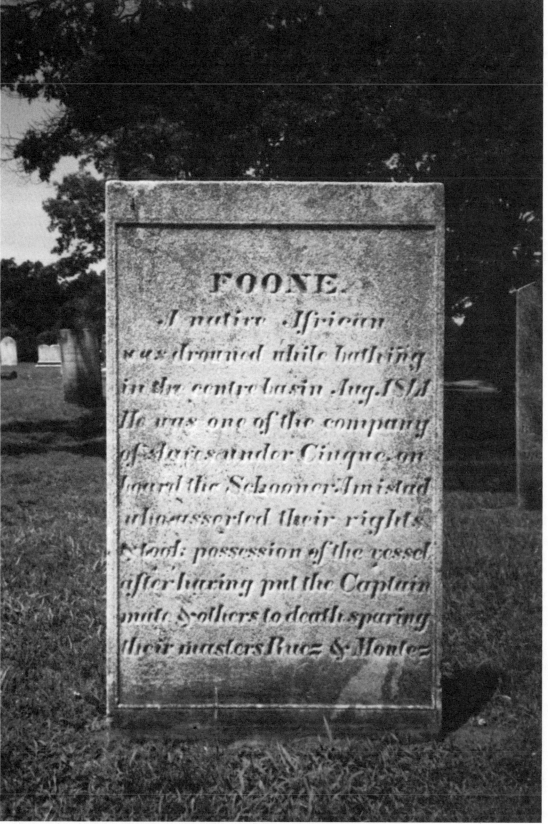

Foone's tombstone in Farmington, Connecticut

unopened grave of slavery in the United States."

The lower court decided that the Mendis were entitled to their freedom. This verdict was upheld by the District Court. But the people who were in favor of slavery felt that they could not let this verdict stand. They appealed to the Supreme Court of the United States. There, John Quincy Adams and Roger Sherman Baldwin pleaded in defense of the Mendis. On March 9, 1841, Justice Story announced that the Supreme Court had agreed with the lower courts that the Mendis should go free.

While their case was dragging through the courts, the Mendis had been confined in New Haven. After they had been granted their freedom, Lewis Tappan of New York, and A. F. Williams and John Norton of Farmington, made arrangements to lodge them in Farmington until they could be returned to Africa. When the worthy citizens of Farmington learned about this, many were somewhat less than enthusiastic about having the Mendis in town. They had heard that these Africans were cannibals, and they did not look forward to the possibility of being barbecued by cannibals in the shadow of their own homes. A barge brought the Mendis up the Farmington Canal from New Haven. Within a short time their quiet dignity and courtesy won the respect and affection of most of those who had at first objected to their coming.

When the Mendis arrived in Farmington, they numbered thirty-seven, including three young girls. A year later thirty-six left town to be established in a colony known as the Mendi Mission in Sierra Leone, Africa.

The one who would never return to his homeland was Foone. He lost his life in the Centre Basin, a place in the Farmington Canal where barges could be moored or turned around. No one knows how it happened. It may have been an accident, but it was not easy to drown in the canal, where the water was not much more than four feet deep. Foone was known to be very homesick for his beloved Africa. Perhaps he could not wait to get home.

For some time, many people in Connecticut had been opposed to the slave trade. Now the Amistad affair stirred even more widespread feeling against slavery, and in 1848 the Connecticut General Assembly passed a law freeing all slaves in the state. At that time Connecticut had only six persons who were being held as slaves.

Chapter Fourteen

Connecticut's Part In The Civil War

If people throughout the United States had believed as Connecticut citizens did in 1861, there would here been no Civil War. Thirteen years earlier the Connecticut General Assembly had passed a law which freed all the slaves in the state. Connecticut did not like the idea of war between the states. Many families had friends and relatives in the South. Some schools had boys and girls who came from southern states. Connecticut businessmen traded with the South. Connecticut people felt that slavery could be abolished in other states as it had been in their own, without bloodshed.

Harriet Beecher Stowe, who was born in Litchfield, expressed her feelings about slavery when she wrote the book, Uncle Tom's Cabin. This story, which told about the Negroes in the South, was read far and wide. It was even printed in more than twenty different languages. After reading the book, many people wanted once and for all to end slavery in this country. In 1859 John Brown, who was born in Torrington, was captured and hanged in an attempt to free the slaves at Harper's Ferry, Virginia.

However, in 1861, when the American flag was fired on at Fort Sumter, the people of Connecticut sadly but firmly closed ranks and prepared to fight. William Buckingham, the governor of the state, called for volunteers; thousands answered this call.

No Confederate soldiers ever invaded our state, and no battles were fought on Connecticut soil. But Connecticut soldiers fought in most of the important battles of the war, and Connecticut sailors died at Fort Fisher and Mobile Bay.

Old Connecticut whaling ships played a part in one of the more colorful incidents of the war. Charleston, South Carolina, was one of the busiest southern ports. In spite of the watch that Union warships kept on the entrances to the Charleston harbor, many blockade runners managed to slip in and out, carrying arms and ammunition to the Confederate army.

Someone in Washington suggested that the blockade runners could be stopped if many old ships were sunk in the channels leading into Charleston harbor. It was decided that a fleet of old ships would be gathered, filled with stone, and sunk in the harbor entrances. Connecticut played a part by supplying a number of old whaling ships from New London, Stonington and Mystic.

The ships were loaded with stone to make them sink quickly. For this reason they became known as the Stone Fleet. They were sailed to Charleston and sunk in the harbor channels. Unfortunately, this bright idea did not bring the war to a speedy end. The blockade runners soon learned to steer their ships between the sunken hulks, and the Confederate army continued to receive the supplies it needed to carry on the war.

Imagine a private soldier providing the money to pay his entire regiment for two full months. Such a thing happened in Connecticut during the Civil War. For some reason the

U.S. General Hospital Ft. Monroe Va
January 5, 1865

Dear Sister Jennie

Was a disappointed I did not write to you before. I should have done so but while I was writing to Charly I received orders to go to Ft. Monroe, so I had that afternoon and then went to bed ready to go to Baltimore. Then in the morning I got up very early to take the cars to go to Baltimore. Then while the rest were asleep and... At the cars which was crowded. The first part of the ride was in the...

I hope we shall, but we shall not unless we begin to love God here on earth. Do you not feel sometimes yes often that you would not want God to see all you think and say? But he does, and he knows all that is wrong. If you feel ashamed of them while you can not see Him, how would you feel if you had to go right where you could see Him? You would be afraid because you would feel that you had done wrong. But you have come to this world to live and now we are to get Him our hearts and then He will keep us from sinning against God and will take us to be always with Him when we die. How do you ever give Him your heart? Do you always pray to Him and ask Him to make you His own every child? Then you will ever try to do right and will be happy.

I think if you thought you... should come home again which I do not know as I shall in a long time.

Your affectionate brother
Edwin

Letter from a Connecticut Civil War soldier to his sister, 1865 men of the Seventeenth Regiment, of Fairfield County, received no pay for four months. The soldiers had no money to send home to their families or to pay for things they needed. One member of the regiment was Elias Howe Jr., whose father had invented the sewing machine. Elias Howe was very wealthy. When the men of his regiment failed to receive their pay, he wrote a check for thirty-one thousand dollars so that the soldiers could have some money to spend.

When the Civil War started there were about 471,000 people in Connecticut. Of the 80,000 who were old enough to vote, over 50,000 went to war. More than 20,500 of these died or were reported missing or wounded. Among those killed were two Connecticut generals, John Sedgwick of Cornwall, and Nathanael Lyon of Ashford. Although many Connecticut men helped the northern army win the war, one of the most important was Gideon Welles, who went to Washington to serve as Secretary of the Navy.

At that time all Union warships were made of wood. Early in the war the Union sank and abandoned the Merrimac, one of its own wooden warships. A few months later the Confederates salvaged the Merrimac and rebuilt her. They armed her with heavy guns and covered her with iron armor plate. When news of this ironclad ship reached Washington, Navy officials were alarmed. They knew the armored Merrimac would be able to sink all the Union's wooden warships.

An engineer named John Ericsson designed a different kind of armored warship which he thought might be better than the Merrimac. He called it the Monitor. Its guns were mounted in a revolving turret, and it looked unlike any other warship. He showed a model to the naval officers in Washington, but they did not believe it would float.

Gideon Welles heard about Ericsson's idea. "Tell Ericsson to come and see me right away," said Welles.

Ericsson came and showed him the model. Welles examined it carefully. "I think it will work," he said. "Go ahead and build it as quickly as possible. We will provide the money, and if it is not successful, I will take the blame."

The Monitor was built at Greenport, Long Island. As soon as it was ready, it started for Hampton Roads where many of the Union warships were anchored. The day before the Monitor arrived, the dreaded Merrimac came up from the South. It sank one Union warship and set another afire. Its crew planned to come back the next day and destroy the rest of the Union fleet.

When the Merrimac returned, her crew saw the strange looking Monitor next to the ship they planned to sink first. They laughed and called it a "Yankee cheese box on a raft." But before the Merrimac could move close to her target, the Monitor blocked her path. All day the two ironclad ships fired at each other. The shells bounced off their heavy armor plate and did no harm. At the end of the day neither ship was badly damaged, but the Merrimac had used up most of her gunpowder and shells. She went back to her home port without sinking any more ships, and she never attacked again.

If Gideon Welles had not recognized the value of the Monitor and ordered it built, the Merrimac might have sunk the entire Union fleet. The blockage of southern ports would have been ended for many months, and the northern army might have lost the war.

After four long years, the Civil War finally ended in 1865. President Lincoln had freed the slaves with the Emancipation Proclamation in 1863, the Union was saved, and the men from Connecticut returned home to take up their lives again.

Chapter Fifteen

Connecticut Continues To Grow (1825-1900)

From the earliest days of the Connecticut colony many of the young men had to leave the towns in which they were born and go west. There was not enough land in the state to provide a farm for every family, and until 1790 there were not many other ways in which a man could earn enough to support a family.

The coming of the turnpikes offered new ways of earning a living. The building of the roads provided many jobs for men with ox teams. After the roads were built and the stagecoaches began to roll, drivers and tollgate guards were needed. When the taverns opened their doors to serve the needs of the stagecoach lines, more jobs were created for cooks, waiters, and men to take care of the horses. Stagecoach owners bought many horses from Connecticut farmers. Tavernkeepers bought meat, vegetables, cider and brandy. This gave the farmers money with which they could buy some of the nice things that were being brought from abroad.

As more ships began to sail from Norwich, Middletown, and New Haven, more jobs became available. Building and rigging a large sailing vessel provided many months of work in the shipyard for scores of men. Other men had jobs cutting, hauling and sawing timbers, casting and shaping anchors and other metal fittings, and making sails. It is no wonder that the shipping towns grew faster than the farming villages. They offered many more opportunities for earning a living.

Digging the canals provided work for hundreds of men and ox teams. Most of these men were paid fifty cents to a dollar a day for their labor, hardly enough to support a family. When a canal was finished, barge captains, mule drivers, and lock tenders were needed. Slowly at first, but faster as time went on, Connecticut began to move out of the period when most of its citizens were farmers.

A large increase in new jobs came when the invention of the enclosed breast wheel made it possible to harness the larger rivers of the state. Before the mill wheels could start to turn, men had to dam the rivers and build canals along their banks. Then the factories had to be put up and the machinery installed. Here again, many new jobs were created far from the location of a factory. There were trees to be cut, logs to be sawed, and stones to be quarried before the factory could be built. Iron ore had to be mined and smelted to provide metal for the machines. Teamsters were needed to haul these materials from sawmills, quarries and iron furnaces.

After the factory was built, men were needed to handle the raw materials, operate the machines, and keep the books. Other men were hired to sell the factory's products and pack them for shipment to distant places.

New towns such as Rockville, Winsted, and Pine Meadow sprang up around the new factories. These towns needed doctors, ministers, tailors, shoemakers, and storekeepers as well as people to work in the factories. Taking care of the needs of the factory workers opened many opportunities for people to earn their living in Connecticut. But this is not the whole story. Men who worked in a factory often worked from six o'clock in the morning until six at night. Some of them worked from sunup to sundown, which meant more than twelve hours a day during the summer. They had no time to raise their own vegetables, cut firewood, or take care of a cow. But with the money they earned in the factory they could afford to buy meat, vegetables, milk and butter from nearby farmers. This made it possible for farmers to buy the axes, chairs, clocks, carpets, and other things that were made in the factories or sold at stores in the cities.

Connecticut could not have become a great manufacturing state if it had depended on water power alone to run its factories. Water power had its faults. Sometimes the river would be almost dry in the summer, and there would not be enough water to turn the wheels. Sometimes heavy rains would flood the river, and water would pour through the windows and doors of the factories, which had to be built close to the river. But the greatest fault was that a water-powered factory could not be enlarged. There was a limit to the amount of power that could be developed at any one location on a river. That amount of power might be enough to run a hundred machines, but in most cases the dam could not be raised high enough to provide power for two hundred machines. Thus it was difficult, often impossible, for a water-powered factory to grow.

Men learned that steam engines could turn paddle wheels to move boats when there was no wind. Then they found that a steam engine could be made to move train wheels along iron rails. Later they discovered that steam engines could be used to turn lathes, looms, trip hammers, and other factory machines. This discovery made it possible for Connecticut to make a great leap forward in wealth and population.

When the water power boom started, it seemed that such towns as Collinsville, Yantic, and Falls Village, which had good water power sites, would become the big cities. Then it was learned that steam power was better than water for turning machines. It did not dry up in summer or cause damage when the river was flooded. A steam-powered factory did not even need to be near a river. Most important, a steam-powered factory could grow. If the factory could sell more than one boiler and engine could produce, another boiler and engine could be added to supply power for twice as many machines. Now any town could become a city if coal could be shipped there by boat or freight train. Meriden, Bristol, New Britain, Naugatuck and many other towns began to grow.

Hartford developed as a manufacturing city because Samuel Colt started his revolver factory there. He used Eli Whitney's idea of interchangeable parts, a system used so well by Chauncey Jerome in making clocks. This meant that in each revolver the parts were exactly the same as the corresponding parts in every other revolver produced by the company. The Colt factory not only created jobs for many Hartford people; it also supplied manufacturing experience for some capable men who later started factories of their own.

At the time when many steam-powered factories were getting started, new railroads were reaching into all parts of Connecticut. Building these railroads made many jobs for

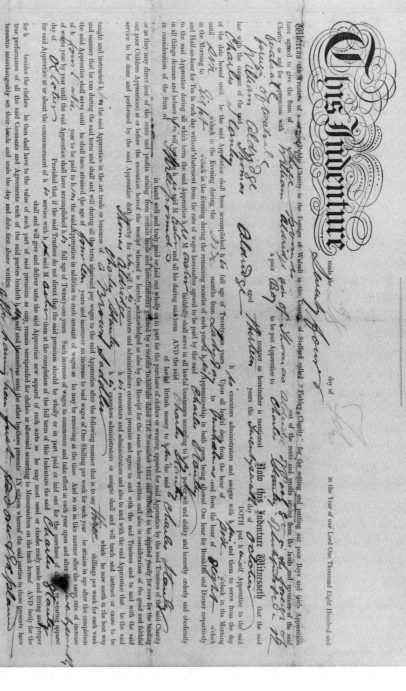

Indenture certificate of William Aldridge, 1874

FISHLEY CHARITY.

Connecticut people, and after they were built, engineers, firemen, brakemen, station agents, conductors and porters were needed to operate them.

As the steam age made hundreds of new jobs available, Connecticut's population began to increase rapidly. The younger sons of farm families no longer had to go west to find a way of earning a living, for Connecticut industries were hiring thousands of workers. People began to come to the state from as far away as Germany, Ireland, Italy, and Poland. Many of them came as indentured servants who were treated almost like slaves. Often the captains of several ships would be competing against one another for passengers leaving Dublin, Bremen, or other European ports.

"My ship will take you to New York for sixty dollars," one captain would say to people who were waiting to come to America.

"I will take you aboard for fifty," another captain would say. Some of the people who wanted to cross the Atlantic had fifty dollars but not much more. They would pay for passage on the less expensive ship. But when the ship reached New York and they got ready to go ashore, the captain would come to them and say, "One hundred dollars, please."

The passenger would reply, "In Dublin you told me the fare to America would be fifty dollars."

"You didn't understand what I said," the captain would argue. "I said you could come aboard for fifty dollars and pay the rest when you reached New York."

Many of these people did not have the additional hundred dollars and did not know where they could borrow the money. They were put into a place called Castle Garden, which was almost as bad as a prison. They were told they would have to stay there until they could pay the hundred dollars.

Soon a stranger would come into Castle Garden and talk to one of the poor immigrants who was wondering how in the world he would ever get out. The man would say, "If you will agree to work for me without pay for two years, I will pay the hundred dollars you owe, and you can get out of here." The poor immigrant would agree to the offer because it seemed that anything would be better than sitting around Castle Garden.

After a year or two the servant would be free. But if he ran away from his master before his term ended, the police would bring him back. Some of those who came as indentured servants were poor boys or girls in Europe, whose fathers had given permission for them to be taken to the United States to become apprentices to skilled tradesmen. The signed agreement specified the daily working hours, the pay, and the number of years that must be served before the young person would be free to change jobs.

The indenture certificate of 13-year-old William Aldridge of England indicates that he was bound, until he reached the age of 21, to work twelve hours a day for Charles Stanley, a saddle maker. William became an expert saddler and spent the rest of his working life making saddles that were truly works of art.

Many of these indentured servants were brought into Connecticut, and some people made them work much longer and harder than they had said they would. The individuals who came to this country as indentured servants contributed much to the development of our state.

The coming of the railroads helped the farmers in many Connecticut towns. As late as 1870 many farmers were still raising or making almost everything they used. Because they had little to sell, they did not have much money. When the railroad came through northwestern Connecticut, creameries were established in many small towns. City people wanted more butter and cheese than the farms near the city could supply. The creameries offered farmers a fair price for all the milk they could produce. The creameries made butter and cheese, which they shipped to the city by rail. Farmers increased their herds and began to receive monthly checks for the milk they sold. That gave them money with which to buy things that were for sale in the stores.

Soon the creameries found that milk stayed fresh longer if the farmer kept it packed with ice while waiting for it to be picked up by the milk collector. They encouraged farmers to build icehouses in which to store ice cut from their ponds during the winter. Farm wives discovered that ice kept meat and other foods fresh and that it could be used to freeze ice cream. As a result, many farm children began to have nicer things to eat. The trolley car was another thing that helped the towns and cities of Connecticut grow in the years before 1900. If a factory owner needed a large number of men to work for him, it must be made easy for them to get from their homes to his factory. In the small mill towns houses clustered around the mill. But when a big factory employed thousands of men, it was not possible for all of them to live close to the factory. The trolley car solved this problem. Soon large towns and cities had streetcar lines running up and down their main streets and out of town to surrounding communities. For a five cent fare a man who lived in West Hartford or Wethersfield could get to his job in the Columbia Bicycle factory or the Hartford Rubber Works in about half an hour. By offering quick and inexpensive transportation the trolley car helped the growth of many Connecticut industries.

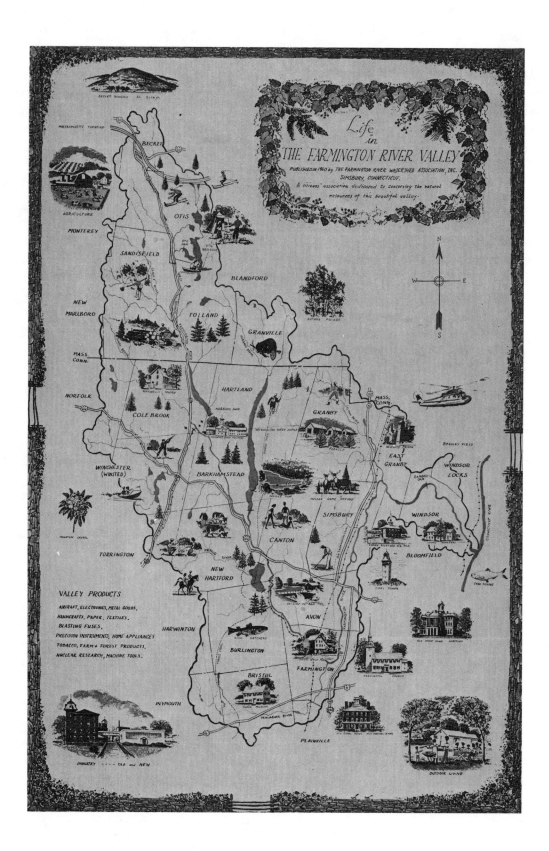

Map of Farmington River Valley

Chapter Sixteen

Wildlife In Connecticut

From the days of the first white settlements in Connecticut, the wild animals of this region have not been a serious menace to people. If any early settler came out second-best in a battle against a bull moose, a brown bear, a catamount or a pack of wolves, the incident was not recorded in our history books. Scores of people have been killed or injured by runaway horses and angry bulls, but the largest wild animals that roamed our forests took their greatest toll among sheep and other livestock. They rarely attempted to make a meal of a Connecticut Yankee.

The wolves that lived in this area were not much larger than foxes. They ran in small packs, usually not more than six. Because they were a menace to sheep, calves, young pigs and poultry, they were soon wiped out by guns, traps or wolf pits. Bears that were native to Connecticut would disappear into the deeper woods when they heard or smelled a man approaching. They would fight if they were cornered or if danger threatened their cubs, but they avoided people whenever possible.

Rattlesnakes and copperheads were probably more dangerous than any of the larger wild creatures. Unlike the bear and the wolf, many of these snakes are still found in the state. Fortunately, they generally inhabit the sun-baked slopes of high rocky ridges where few people are likely to meet them.

When the first European settlers came to Connecticut, almost all of the region was blanketed with trees. These were quickly cleared from the fertile lowlands to make room for fields of wheat and corn. Soon the trees were cut from hilly areas to provide fuel for homes and charcoal for the iron furnaces. By 1750 there were few large forests where deer could find protection. For more than a hundred years there were few if any deer in the state. It seemed that the deer had joined the wolf and the bear as a mere memory of the past.

Then, around 1850, many owners of hill farms began moving west or into the cities. Some of the farms were abandoned, and the forests soon began to reclaim the land that had been cleared. Coal began to take the place of wood for household fuel, and the use of Pennsylvania steel reduced the demand for charcoal to burn in Connecticut iron furnaces. Within a few years great areas of the state were once again covered with trees.

Shortly after the Civil War, on the closing day of a session of the Connecticut General Assembly, someone with a sense of humor proposed a bill that anyone found guilty of shooting a deer should be fined five hundred dollars. That was considered a good joke, for none of the members had ever seen a deer in Connecticut. In a spirit of fun they voted for the bill, and the governor signed it into law.

About twenty-five years later a farmer in a small Connecticut town said to his neighbor, "Saw a strange animal in the pasture with my cows this evening. Feel sure it must have been a deer."

The neighbor looked thoughtfully at his friend but did not reply. That night he remarked to his wife, "I'm afraid Uriah's been drinking too much hard cider lately. He said he'd seen a deer in the pasture with his cows. Doesn't he know that there hasn't been a deer in this town for the past hundred years?"

A few evenings later, however, as the neighbor was driving his horse and buggy to a Grange meeting, he was startled to see a deer bound across the road in front of him. He knew then that the deer had indeed come back to Connecticut. But when he told his wife what he had seen, she asked if he too had had some of Uriah's hard cider.

Deer are often seen today in Connecticut woodlands and fields. Now and then one is struck while crossing a busy highway. Some are killed by hunters. But as long as Connecticut has large wooded areas and marshes, some deer will manage to survive.

The story of the beaver is similar to the story of the deer. In the early years of the Connecticut colony, both Indians and settlers trapped great numbers of beavers. The skins brought a good price, for beaver hats were the popular style in England. By 1750 beavers were scarce in this region, and for many years none were reported seen. Between 1920 and 1940 a few beavers were released along Connecticut streams. Their numbers increased rapidly. Within a few years state authorities began receiving calls for help from people whose land was being flooded. "A family of beavers has built a dam across our brook," one man complained. "The water has backed up over the road leading to our house. Please come and take them away." Many beavers were moved to more remote places where their dams would not cause trouble for land owners.

The mocking bird and certain others that once lived farther south have made themselves at home in Connecticut. However, the osprey, the bald eagle and the passenger pigeon, which were once common in the state, are rarely or never seen here now.

Perhaps, because it involves a mystery, the most interesting of these is the passenger pigeon. Until about 1885 large flocks of these birds were seen here and elsewhere in the United States. The flocks were so large that they would blot out the sun as they passed overhead, and it sometimes took hours for a flock to pass any one place. At times they were a nuisance. When they stopped to rest at night they often roosted so close together that their weight broke limbs from the trees. If they happened to drop in on a farmer's grape arbor or blueberry patch, it would take them less than five minutes to eat every bit of fruit from the vines or bushes. Millions of these birds were shot or netted. Connecticut farmers sent barrels of them to the markets, where they were sold for a few cents each. But the hunters seemed to have little effect on the number of passenger pigeons. The flocks returning south each fall seemed larger than those that had come north in the spring.

In the spring of 1888, the year of the great blizzard, few pigeons came to Connecticut. Some people thought the huge flocks might have been smothered in the blizzard. Others said they must have gone to different parts of the country. But other states reported that they too had very few passenger pigeons that year. By 1890 these birds had just about disappeared, and not one has been seen in Connecticut since 1900.

The passenger pigeon left no clue to the reason for his disappearance. Some people blamed the hunters. Others thought a great storm might have blown the huge flocks so far out over the sea that they dropped into the water and drowned, exhausted by their efforts to get back to land. Another possibility is that the passenger pigeon was exterminated by disease rather than by violence. When a disease is spread to a part of the world where the people, animals or plants have built up no resistance against it, a whole species of living things may be destroyed. The chestnut blight is an example of such a disease. It was brought to our shores from a foreign land, and within a short time it had spread throughout the state. Since 1910 every mature chestnut tree in Connecticut has been killed by the blight.

Although we do not know why the passenger pigeon is no longer seen in our skies, we do know why another Connecticut visitor, the Atlantic salmon, has disappeared from our rivers. The early settlers found that every spring brought millions of salmon surging out of Long Island Sound into the rivers of our state. The Housatonic, the Connecticut and the Thames were filled with salmon, some weighing as much as fifty pounds. The Atlantic salmon, along with shad, lamprey eels, alewives and sturgeon, pushed their way to spawning grounds in the clear gravelly reaches of the upper tributaries of the rivers. There they laid their eggs.

If our rivers had not provided such a plentiful supply of fish, there would have been few Indians in interior Connecticut. There was not enough wild game in the forests to feed all the tribes who lived along the river valleys. Fortunately, most of the fish that came in from the sea did not need to find food while they were in the fresh water. Before they began their journey to the spawning grounds their bodies had stored a rich supply of proteins and oils. If it had been necessary for them to feed in the rivers, they might have eaten all the young fish they had spawned in previous years.

Millions of salmon swam up our rivers in 1630, but today there are few. Atlantic salmon insist on laying their eggs in the same clear, swift-flowing water where they themselves were spawned. If anything prevents them from reaching their spawning beds, they return to the sea without laying their eggs. When the early settlers began to dam rivers and streams to provide water power for their mills, they made it impossible for many fish to reach their original spawning grounds. The people did not realize that their dams would discourage the fish from coming up the rivers. They did not know that salmon would lay their eggs only in their own special spawning beds. If the settlers had understood the habits of salmon, they would have built fish ladders to help the fish get over the dams, for salmon provided an important source of food.

Shad still swim up some of our rivers to spawn. They do not insist on finding a particular place to lay their eggs. They are satisfied to spawn in any part of the river where the water is swift and shallow. Fish ladders have been built at the dams in some of our rivers, making it possible for the shad to reach new spawning grounds. As a result, the spring run of shad is likely to increase in future years.

In 1600 there were not as many different kinds of wild flowers in Connecticut as there are today. Almost all of the state was covered with trees. When the leaves came out on the trees, the ground became so shady that most flowers could not get enough sunlight to bring out their blossoms. The most common wild flowers were arbutus, hepatica, bloodroot and other early varieties which bloomed before the trees were fully leafed out in the spring.

Many of our field flowers which bloom in late spring or summer are not native to Connecticut. They were brought here from Europe. They were first planted in the gardens of the early settlers. Some seeds were carried beyond the garden walls, perhaps by children, birds or the wind. In our climate and soil they were able to grow without cultivation, and each year new seeds were spread over wider areas. Some of our common wild flowers came originally from seeds that were mixed with the wheat and oats which the settlers brought from England. When the early farmers sowed the grain they also scattered the seeds of these English field flowers.

Wild flowers add great beauty to the Connecticut countryside, but some of them are in danger of disappearing forever. As our population grows, lawns and shopping centers replace fields and woodlands. Some wild flowers will not bloom again if their blossoms are picked. When the flower is picked from a pink lady-slipper or a trout-lily, the plant suffers such a shock that it may not bloom again for several years. Some kinds of flowers will die out unless their seeds are sowed every year. When the blossoms are picked no seeds can ripen.

We can help preserve the beauty of Connecticut by protecting our wild life. Instead of hunting animals and birds with guns, or picking the blossoms from wild flowers, we can hunt with cameras. Photography is a fascinating hobby, and beautiful pictures are far more enjoyable than dead animals or wilted flowers.

Chapter Seventeen

Reading, Writing And Arithmetic

Connecticut's early settlers knew the importance of learning to read and write. In 1641 New Haven established the first school in the state, and in 1643 the second school was started in Hartford. Since there were no separate school buildings, classes were held at the home of the schoolmaster. Only boys attended the earliest schools, but when the towns began to control their own schools, both boys and girls were allowed to attend.

In the years before 1800 most boys planned to be farmers, and they saw little need for many years of study. There were no agricultural colleges, for people thought that working on a farm was the best way to learn about farming. Thus, during Connecticut's first century and a half, few towns offered anything more than one-room schools where reading, writing and arithmetic were taught.

The one-room schools were often crude and uncomfortable. Usually they had separate playgrounds and separate entrances for boys and girls. They were hard to heat in winter. The seats were hard benches, and the desks were long rough boards fastened to the wall. The pupils had few books and no blackboards, colored pictures, maps or globes. Pens were made of goose quills sharpened by the teacher. A birch rod or a hickory stick was used to punish any child who did not behave.

These country schools depended almost entirely on the teacher. None had the many aids to education found in the schools of today. But they had some advantages. There were no clearly defined grades. A student could listen to the older children recite their lessons and learn from them. He did not have to wait for promotion to do advanced work. A slow learner, on the other hand, did not have to struggle desperately to keep up with his class. He could stay in the school learning as much as he could absorb until he was able to do simple jobs on the farm.

Before the Civil War most of the teachers were men. People were afraid a woman teacher might have trouble with some of the unruly or older boys. When the Civil War broke out and many schoolmasters volunteered to fight, some schools were left without teachers. To avoid closing the schools, women were hired to teach. They did such a good job that Connecticut has had many women teachers since that time.

There were no buses to carry children to the early schools. Almost every town had a number of small schools located so that most farms in the town would be within walking distance of a school. Walking distance was generally considered to be not more than two miles.

For many years parents had to pay part of the teacher's salary, and some families could not afford to send their children to school. Sometimes families would pay their share of school costs by having the teacher live with them for a week or two for each child they had in school. Many boys attended school only during the winter, when there was not so much farm work to be done. Few children continued to go to school after they were fourteen or fifteen years old.

Those who wished to increase their knowledge found ways to continue their education. If a boy wanted to go to Yale and become a minister, he would find someone to tutor him. If he wanted to be an architect, he might become an apprentice to a builder and study all the available books about architecture. A boy who wanted to study medicine would learn from a local doctor. Perhaps he would agree to take care of the doctor's horse and do other chores. In return, the doctor would teach the boy all he knew about medicines and taking care of patients. After a few years the young man could start treating sick people himself. Before Tapping Reeve started America's first law school at Litchfield in 1784, lawyers were trained in somewhat the same way. A young man would go into a lawyer's office and "read law" for several years. He would tend the fires and sweep the floors to pay for his training.

Many young men became apprentices to printers, cabinetmakers, or other skilled craftsmen. During the seven years of their apprenticeship they worked hard and learned their trades well.

Strange as it may seem, during the first half of the nineteenth century Connecticut schools suffered because of too much help from the state. Under the terms of its charter, Connecticut owned about a thousand square miles of land west of Pennsylvania. In 1795 the land was sold for $1,200,000. The interest from this money, about $60,000 a year, was paid to the towns to help support the schools. Before this happened people had been taxing themselves to pay for the schools in their town, and they had made sure that their tax money was wisely used. But when the state began to pay a large part of school expenses the landowners were no longer heavily taxed, and they lost interest in the schools. Little care was given to finding good teachers, school terms were shortened, buildings were neglected, and teachers were very poorly paid. Some of the men who taught received only $14.50 per month, and women were paid as little as $5.75 per month.

The district schools were growing worse at the very time when there was a great need for better education. New industries were being started in Connecticut. New methods of travel were developing. Men needed education and training for many of the new jobs which were becoming available.

In the years before the Revolution the county towns, such as Litchfield, Tolland, Fairfield and Windham, had maintained Latin schools. These were similar to high schools. Now, when few people seemed to care about the schools, some of the Latin schools were allowed to close. Others were badly neglected.

However, in most Connecticut towns there were people who wanted their children to have a good education. They understood the growing need for more knowledge. To provide for this need academies were established. Academies were private schools. Some were started by Yale graduates who wanted to make good use of their college training. Most academies began as day schools, and many would take a pupil of any age and continue his education until he was ready for college. Some of the academies became so widely known as good schools that pupils came from out of town and out of state. Soon the number of students living at the school was greater than the number coming from home each day. Miss Porter's School in Farmington and Suffield Academy were among these early private schools.

Before long, people decided to do something about the poor quality of the public schools. They began to realize that democracy would not work well unless most of the voters had enough education to understand what was going on in their town, their state and the country. They saw that many important jobs could not be filled by people who were poorly educated. Taxpayers in the school districts began to spend more money to improve teaching and repair school buildings. In later years high schools were established, free textbooks were supplied, and additional books were made available through libraries. Gradually the public school system grew and improved.

Many Connecticut people have spent their lives working to provide better education. Henry Barnard's influence was felt throughout the nation. As one result of his firm belief in public education, and through the cooperation of Catherine Beecher, Samuel May, Emma Hart Willard and others, the first state school for training teachers was established in New Britain in 1849. Known for many years as New Britain Normal School, it later became a state college and its name was changed to Central Connecticut State College, now University.

Since the end of the Civil War, education in Connecticut has grown rapidly. At that time the only colleges in the state were Yale, Trinity and Wesleyan, and there were few free public high schools. Now Connecticut colleges enroll thousands of students, and boys and girls in every town are entitled to a free public education through high school.

Forbes iron furnace at East Canaan, Connecticut

Chapter Eighteen

Vanished Industries – Whaling And Iron

The early settlers of Connecticut found many ways of supplying most of the things they needed. But many years passed before they had a light that was good enough to read by at night. They used tallow or bayberry candles, and some people had crude oil lamps, called Betty lamps. Betty lamps gave light that was little better than candlelight. They made a lot of smoke that had a very unpleasant smell.

Then someone invented a new kind of lamp. It had a glass chimney to keep the flame from flickering, and a small round screen under the chimney to supply the flame with air. This invention was good news for people who wanted to read at night, but it was bad news for whales. The new lamp burned oil. No one had yet discovered petroleum, the oil that comes from under the ground. Oil from coconuts, olives, and palm trees was not produced in Connecticut. There was no cheap vegetable oil that could be used, but there were whales in the waters off our coast.

There had been some demand for whale oil before the new lamp was invented, but when people began to use the new lamps the demand for whale oil increased. Whales became valuable. Men spent a great deal of money for ships, harpoons, and other equipment needed on whaling ships.

Whaling ships were built at many places along our rivers and shore. Noank, Stonington, Essex, and Middle Haddam were among the towns where ships were built for hunting whales. New London, Mystic and Stonington were the ports from which most of the Connecticut whalers sailed.

At first there were plenty of whales in nearby waters, and whaling voyages were short. When these waters had been depleted, a whaler might be away from her port a year or two before she was able to fill her casks with oil.

Hunting whales was a dangerous business. High on the mast of the whaling ship, the lookout kept watch. When he sighted a whale, he would call to the captain. Whaleboats would be launched, and the men would row toward the whale. Sometimes the boats would be swamped in a rough sea. Sometimes a wounded whale would smash a boat. Rarely did a whaling ship return to Mystic or New London with as many men aboard as when she had left port.

After a whale had been killed, it would be brought alongside the whaler. The blubber would be cut off in big chunks and hauled up to the deck. There, in big kettles over open fires, it would be cooked to get out the oil. After most of the oil had been cooked out and stored, the remainder of the blubber was used for fuel. It burned with a black, oily smoke. Everybody and everything aboard a whaler soon became black from the oily soot.

For many years the whaling industry provided jobs for thousands of men in southeastern Connecticut. All the jobs were not on the whaling ships. Men worked at building the ships, making sails and other equipment, refining the whale oil, and selling supplies the whalers needed for their long voyages.

We may wonder why such a profitable industry died. The Civil War did not help the whaling industry. When the navy was building up the Stone Fleet to block Charleston harbor, it paid high prices for old ships. Some of the Mystic, New London and Stonington whalers became part of the Stone Fleet and were sunk in the entrances to Charleston harbor. Many more were captured by Confederate commerce raiders. The Alabama and the Shenandoah counted many whaling ships among their victims. One unfortunate incident was the sinking or burning of many whaling ships in the Bering Sea months after the war had ended. Neither the skipper of the Shenandoah, the Confederate raider which attacked the whalers, nor any of the whaling captains knew that the fighting had ended. None of them had been in a port for months, and this was long before the invention of radio, which today keeps a ship's crew informed of the news.

The whaling industry probably would have survived the damage it suffered in the Civil War, but something more important happened. Oil was discovered in Pennsylvania, and one of the many valuable products which can be made from petroleum is kerosene.

Kerosene gave a brighter light than whale oil. It did not smoke or smell fishy. Most important of all, it was less expensive. Five gallons of kerosene cost about as much as one gallon of whale oil. For a number of years, Connecticut people did their reading at night by the light of kerosene lamps. Later, gas and electricity came into common use. They produced brighter, cheaper and cleaner light. Today most kerosene lamps are considered antiques.

Iron mining and smelting, another of Connecticut's vanished industries, had a longer life than the whaling industry. It started about 1770, just a few years before the Revolution. It lasted until about 1920, just a few years after World War I. But today one of these industries is as dead as the other. There are no more tons of iron ore being mined in Salisbury than there are barrels of whale oil being brought into New London.

There is still a large body of very good iron ore in northwestern Connecticut. As a matter of fact, it extends from Connecticut across western Massachusetts and into Vermont. It makes a fine grade of iron. The ore is soft and breaks up easily. In most places it lies close to the surface of the ground. Therefore, it would not be necessary to blast holes in the rock or to go deep underground to mine this ore.

Salisbury iron helped the American colonies win the Revolution. It was used in cannon and bayonets that helped the North win the Civil War. When railroad tracks were made of Salisbury iron, they were the strongest kind of iron rails. Even after steel had pushed it out of many markets, Salisbury iron was still used to make a train wheel so tough that it would not crack, with a hard shell that would not easily dent or wear away.

Again, we may wonder why such an industry died out while there was still plenty of ore to be mined. There are several reasons. Salisbury iron was smelted with charcoal. Many bushels of charcoal were needed to smelt a ton of pig iron. It took a great number of trees to provide those bushels of charcoal. First the ironmasters used the trees that were near their furnaces. New trees grew slowly, and by 1900 the ironmasters had to go fifty or sixty miles to get charcoal. Hauling charcoal was costly. It could not be carried in railroad cars; sparks from the steam locomotives might set it afire.

But the high cost of charcoal alone would not have killed the Connecticut iron industry. The ironmasters could have continued to raise their prices, unless the people who needed iron were able to buy it somewhere else at a lower cost. It was the same old story. The railroads drove the stagecoaches out of business because they offered faster, more comfortable, and less expensive transportation. The oil wells put the whalers out of business because kerosene burned brighter and cost less than whale oil. Starting in the 1870s, steel began to push Connecticut iron out of the market. For many uses, steel was better and cheaper than iron.

Why could steel, which requires more processing, be made at a lower price than our iron? Mountains of iron ore were discovered in Minnesota. The area was known as the "Mesabi Range." This ore could be mined by steam shovels and dumped into freight cars which rolled downhill to Duluth. There it was.poured into big steamboats and hauled across the lakes to furnaces on the lake shores of Ohio and Indiana. Because it could be handled in large quantities by machinery, it cost less to haul a ton of ore all this distance than it cost to load a ton of ore into a wagon at Salisbury and haul it eight miles to the iron furnaces at East Canaan or Lime Rock.

This was not the whole story. The Indiana and Ohio furnaces used coke instead of charcoal to smelt the ore. Enough coke to smelt a ton of iron cost much less than enough charcoal to do the same job. This helped make the Mesabi iron far less expensive than Connecticut iron. Perhaps most important of all, Connecticut iron made excellent wrought iron, but it did not make good steel. Steel was cheaper than wrought iron, and it was much better for building railroads, skyscrapers and big bridges.

Some of the old iron furnaces can still be found at East Canaan, Lime Rock, and Huntsville. Some of the dams which produced power needed for smelting iron ore now make very pretty waterfalls, but the furnace stacks have crumbled, and trees are growing where the casting sheds once stood.

Early automobile in trouble on a muddy road

P. J. HOLDEN

Chapter Nineteen

Automobiles And Electric Power – Two Things That Have Changed Our Lives

The map of Connecticut was changed by the discovery that a steam engine could turn factory wheels. Many small villages began to expand into cities. Wherever coal could be delivered at low cost, a factory could be started. If it produced something people needed, at a price they could pay, it would grow. No longer would its growth be limited by the volume of water in a nearby river. As the factory grew, the surrounding town grew even faster.

Before 1910 most factories were box-shaped buildings with three or four floors. This was because the machines had to be as close as possible to the steam engine that provided power. Belts from the engine turned shafts which extended the full length of a factory room. Belts from these shafts transferred power to each machine.

It was very important that the factory be near a railroad in order to reduce the cost of handling materials. If coal could be dumped from a freight car into a bin near the boiler room, it was less expensive than hauling coal across the town by horse and wagon. The same was true of raw materials and finished products. The less they had to be moved, the lower the costs were.

The population of factory towns increased rapidly. People who worked in the factories liked to live within walking distance of their jobs.

More changes were brought about by a later discovery. Men found that steam and water turbines could be made to turn huge generators which would produce electricity at a very low cost. Electricity could run motors, and the motors could turn machines. This was important. It meant that the factory no longer had to be near the railroad to get an inexpensive power supply. Electricity travels through wires which can go almost anywhere. The factory no longer needed to be designed like a three-story box. The electric motors did away with the big shafts and belts. If the factory owners decided to buy their electricity instead of making it themselves, they no longer needed the steam engines, boilers, and tall chimneys.

While these changes were taking place in the factories, equally important things were happening in other places. The automobile began to take the place of the horse, and electric power started to flow into many homes.

For some years after factory owners learned that the electric motor could do a better job than the steam engine, they still clung to their old box-like buildings along the railroad tracks. They had a lot of money invested in the old factories. If they put up a new one-floor plant out in the country where they could find plenty of space, how would their workers get there? It would be too far to walk, and most trolley lines did not go far enough to provide transportation. Not until the late 1940s was this problem solved. By that time almost everybody could afford to own a car. The Connecticut industries and businesses began to move from their cramped quarters in the cities to the wide open spaces where there was room to make the most efficient use of machines and equipment. The workers liked the new plants, and there was plenty of room to park their cars.

For a great many years people from foreign countries streamed into Connecticut to fill any jobs that were available. Men and women from Germany, Ireland, Italy, Poland and other parts of the world were willing to wash dishes, work looms, or do the pick and shovel work on the canals, railroads, and highways. These people helped the state make steady growth in population between 1840 and 1940. Later, many workers came from Maine, Vermont, and other states. Connecticut aircraft, submarine, and insurance companies were growing. They offered wages that attracted many men who had been trying to make a living on worn-out farms.

Industry was not the only thing to be changed by the coming of electric power and the automobile. Our homes and towns were also changed. No longer is it necessary to live within walking distance of work. Now it is possible to live among the wooded hills in the eastern or western part of the state, or in a pretty little town near the shore, and commute daily to an office or factory many miles away. Connecticut people can live in the country and still enjoy the comforts and conveniences of the city. Electric power has brought automatic heat, running water, refrigeration, light, and entertainment into almost every home in Connecticut. Few homes in the state are now more than fifteen minutes by automobile from the nearest shopping center. Most small towns within twenty-five miles of a large city have doubled or tripled their population. Now it is often hard to tell where one town ends and another begins.

The automobile has brought about many changes in our lives. During the early 1900s there were very few automobiles in Connecticut, and most of those were used around the cities. Outside the cities there were usually only dirt roads, which were dusty in summer and quite impassable when the frost was coming out of the ground in spring. All through the winter both city streets and country roads were allowed to remain covered with snow to keep them good for sleighing. Most automobile owners put away their cars from Thanksgiving until Easter. A cold engine was hard to start when it had to be cranked by hand.

Now almost every family has at least one car. Towns and cities are linked by thousands of miles of smooth highways. People travel great distances for both business and social reasons. Children learn more about their state by visiting its beaches, parks, mountains, libraries, museums, and historical landmarks.

Chapter Twenty

The Present Grows Out Of The Past

Until the end of the Civil War Connecticut was quite self-sufficient. Connecticut fields produced enough food for the people and their livestock. Home-grown materials provided clothing. Houses were built and heated with wood from the forests, and whale oil brought into Mystic, Stonington and New London supplied plenty of fuel for lamps. Connecticut had its own iron industry. Its rivers and brooks provided power for mills which did much of the work that could not be easily done by hand.

Today Connecticut farms produce a good supply of poultry, eggs, milk, fruits and vegetables. But Connecticut must depend on other states to provide grain, meat, cloth, fuels, metals, lumber and many manufactured products. Most of the fish eaten in Connecticut comes from Boston and New York markets. The state still has a number of good harbors, but Stonington is about the only port where many commercial fishing vessels are likely to be seen. If all the bridges and tunnels across the Hudson River were suddenly destroyed, Connecticut people would begin to feel hungry within a week.

If Connecticut no longer produces so many of the things it needs, we may wonder how these things are made available to the people of our state. Connecticut businesses and industries sell many products and services to people in other parts of the country. Much of the money received by these companies is paid to their workers and stockholders, who use part of the money to buy meat, flour, automobiles, gasoline, and other things that are not generally produced here. Thus the money a Kansas farmer pays for Connecticut insurance may be used by insurance company employees to pay for beef that is raised in Kansas and sold in Connecticut meat markets.

Many people invest money in the stocks of companies located in other states. For example, a Connecticut man may invest some of his savings in a copper mining company in Arizona, and that company may pay him a dividend every three months. The man may deposit his dividends in a local bank, and eventually the bank may lend the money to a Connecticut businessman who needs to buy some copper from Arizona. In this way the use of money makes it possible for people in our state to exchange products and services with the people of other states. Thousands of people have full-time jobs in advertising, selling and buying. Their work promotes a steady exchange of money, materials and finished products.

One of Connecticut's nicknames, "Nutmeg State," can probably be traced to our first traveling salesmen. These Yankee peddlers had a reputation for being shrewd traders, sometimes too shrewd. It is said that some of them spent long winter evenings carving wooden nutmegs; as they traveled through the countryside in their red wagons loaded with hundreds of household items, they sold the wooden nutmegs along with real ones. This story may have been started by someone who had been outsmarted by a Yankee peddler. The products and services of Connecticut industries have long been sold throughout the world; if customers were being cheated, they would soon stop doing business with Connecticut firms.

Connecticut is also known as the "Land of Steady Habits." This name reflects the purpose and character of the founders of our state. They settled in the wilderness, where they established a society based on their faith in God and their faith in themselves. They were proud and independent, but they valued the lessons learned from experience. Through many generations Connecticut people have passed along to their sons and daughters a great respect for the accomplishments of the past, for education, independent thinking and hard work. The steady habits of its citizens have been largely responsible for Connecticut's economic growth. Perhaps our state can best serve its people and the country by continuing to be a "Land of Steady Habits."

The official nickname of Connecticut, adopted by the legislature in 1959, is "Constitution State." Although Connecticut was not the only state whose government provided some guidelines for the United States Constitution, the Fundamental Orders of 1639 contained ideas which certainly had an influence on the organization of the federal government. The Connecticut delegates to the convention which drew up the American Constitution were three able and experienced lawyers: Roger Sherman of New Haven, Oliver Ellsworth of Windsor, and Samuel Johnson of Stratford. Their wisdom and their firm belief in Connecticut's principles of self-government were a powerful force in the convention of 1787. Through the ideals and hard work of many of its early citizens Connecticut earned the name of "Constitution State."

Chapter Twenty-One

Connecticut: Government By Consent Of The Governed

In 1639 Thomas Hooker helped draw up a set of rules that established self-government for the people of Connecticut. Since that time citizens of the state have continued to govern themselves.

In a small town the people make the rules by which the town is governed. They go to town meetings and vote for or against any changes or new regulations that are introduced. The first selectman is the chief officer of a small town. His job is to enforce the laws of the town and to see that the roads are kept in good condition and the people's tax money is wisely spent. The first selectman is elected by the voters.

In a larger town or city, the chief officer elected by the people may be a mayor. All the voters in a city cannot crowd into the city hall for a town meeting. Therefore, the laws and regulations are laid down by the city council, whose members are elected by the people. In some cities the council has the power to choose a city manager instead of a mayor. In such cities the voters have to rely on the wisdom of the council members, for the people do not vote directly for the city manager.

The state government is somewhat similar to that of the towns. The governor is elected by the people. He chooses the men who will collect the taxes, supervise the building of highways, and enforce the laws of the state. The General Assembly, whose members are elected by the voters of the state, passes laws and levies taxes.

There have been some important changes in Connecticut's government since the Fundamental Orders were drawn up in 1639. Each town no longer sends four representatives to the General Assembly. The number of representatives from a particular area is based on its present population. No longer is the governor elected for a one-year term and obliged to wait at least one year before being reelected to the same office. Now the governor's term is four years, and he may be reelected immediately. The original General Assembly was made up of one house and included magistrates appointed by the governor. The two houses in our present General Assembly are the Senate and the House of Representatives. All members of both houses are elected by the voters. Women and blacks, who were not allowed to vote in the early days, have been casting their ballots for many years.

In spite of these and other changes, Connecticut's government is still based on Thomas Hooker's idea that government should be by consent of the governed. Many years ago this idea spread across our borders and swept over and beyond the North American continent. Today millions of people in all parts of the world are enjoying the benefits of self-government, and other millions are struggling to obtain those benefits.

Successful self-government depends upon good citizens. A good citizen must help choose capable and honest people to govern his town, state, and country. He must be willing to serve in public office if people think he is the best person for the job, even when he might be able to earn more money in some other job. If he is called for military service or jury duty, he must do his best to serve well. He must obey the laws and pay his taxes. He must keep informed about the work being done by his elected representatives so he can support the men and measures that seem to be best for his town and state.

Under a successful system of self-government, wise leaders and good citizens promote steady economic growth of the state through continuous development of all its resources. The most important resources are the people themselves, who must use their knowledge to develop all other resources. Yankee ingenuity and inventiveness have created hundreds of industries in the state, many of which were the first of their kind in the country or even in the world. Many Connecticut industries have expanded to establish branches in other states and other countries. Now manufacturing, technology and commerce provide the basis for much of the state's prosperity, for Connecticut is one of the principal industrial centers in the United States.

Connecticut citizens continue to use their skill and training to develop new ideas, products, materials and methods. Improvements are being made in the appearance and usefulness of buildings, land and roads in most Connecticut cities and towns. Transportation and communication facilities are constantly being made more efficient. As these changes create more jobs, the state's population increases; it is as true now as it was in the days of the Indians that the greatest numbers of people can live where there are the greatest numbers of opportunities for earning a living.

While Connecticut citizens enjoy the benefits of these and other developments, they also have a duty to make certain that their government continues to serve the people of the state and the nation. We cannot enjoy the rights and freedoms of self-government without also accepting the responsibilities of citizenship.

BIBLIOGRAPHY

l. Barber, J. W., <u>History of the Amistad Captives</u>, published 1840.

2. Barnum, P. T., <u>40 Years Recollections</u>, American News, New York, 1871.

3. Clark, George L., <u>A History of Connecticut,</u> Knickerbocker Press, New York, 1914.

4. Collins, Samuel W., <u>Recollections of Samuel W. Collins</u>, unpublished manuscript written between 1867 and 1870.

5. Dayton, F. E., <u>Steamboat Days</u>, F. A. Slokes Co., New York, 1925.

6. DeForest, John W., <u>History of the Indians of Connecticut</u> W. J. Hamerseley, Hartford, Conn., 1852.

7. <u>Founders and Leaders of Connecticut, 1633-1783,</u> edit. by Charles Edward Perry, D. C. Heath and Co., New York, 1934.

8. Gay, Julius, <u>Farmington Papers,</u> series of lectures given at Farmington Library Assoc. Some were published in <u>Farmington, a Village of Beautiful Homes,</u> by A. L. Brandegee and E. M. Smith in 1906.

9. Harlow, A. F., <u>Steelways of New England,</u> Creative Age Press, New York, 1946.

10. "Hartford Courant", 200th Anniversary Edition, published by The Hartford Courant, Hartford, Conn., Oct. 18, 1964.

11. Mills, Lewis S., <u>The Story of Connecticut</u>, Charles Scribner's Sons, New York, 1932.

12. "State of Connecticut Register and Manual", published by State of Conn., Hartford, 1964.

13. "Tercentenary Commission of the State of Connecticut", Publications on Conn. 3 Volumes (60 pamphlets), New Haven, Yale University Press, 1934.

14. Twitchell, Willis I.,<u>Hartford in History</u>, Plimpton Mfg. Co., Hartford, 1907.

15. Woodward, Henry P., <u>Insurance in Connecticut</u>.